The Referee's a W****r

The Referee's a W*****r

THE GOOD, THE BAD AND THE DOWNRIGHT OFFENSIVE – BRITAIN'S MOST FAMOUS FOOTBALL CHANTS

ALEX SHAW

FOREWORD BY JEFF WINTER

JB

JOHN BLAKE

Published by John Blake Publishing Ltd,
3 Bramber Court, 2 Bramber Road,
London W14 9PB, England

www.johnblakepublishing.co.uk

First published in hardback in 2010

ISBN: 978-1-84454-889-7

British Library Cataloguing-in-Publication Data:

A catalogue record for this book is available from the British Library.

Design by www.envydesign.co.uk

Printed in Great Britain by
CPI William Clowes Ltd, Beccles, NR34 7TL

1 3 5 7 9 10 8 6 4 2

Papers used by John Blake Publishing are natural, recyclable products made
from wood grown in sustainable forests. The manufacturing processes
conform to the environmental regulations of the country of origin.

Every attempt has been made to contact the relevant copyright-holders,
but some were unobtainable. We would be grateful if the appropriate people
could contact us.

To Mum, Dad, Jenny and Jodie

CONTENTS

ACKNOWLEDGEMENTS

I would like to give my thanks to Nick and Gerry and all the lads at Hayters Sports Agency for not only giving me a job but for putting up with me as well. In writing this book I must say thank you to all the football club press offices and historians who have pointed me in the right direction of a good song or story, as well as a smattering of club message boards with a whole host of funny songs. Work experience students from Brighton University have played their part too, as well as Allie Collins at Blake for always being on hand to help me out with any query I had.

And lastly, thank you to Ole Gunnar Solskjaer: Who put the ball in the Germans' net!?

FOREWORD
by Jeff Winter

'The Referee's a wanker' – that always puzzled me. The best chants are the humorous ones and those that are original. My favourite was 'Oh, Graham Poll is a fucking arsehole' – which was funny and, some might say, quite true.

You have to smile and not let the chants get to you. Once I was reffing at St. James's Park. Newcastle were playing Blackburn Rovers and the away fans started chanting 'You don't know what you're doing'. Then the Newcastle fans joined in. I had to laugh – they couldn't all be wrong, could they!

The amount of pressure and media coverage surrounding referees nowadays is such that hearing a chant or two from the stands is like water off a duck's back. In fact, if a ref is being abused by the fans or players of a particular side then you have to wonder how that might affect his next decision. By

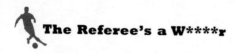

getting that frustration off their chests, fans could actually be adding to their team's problems.

Ref bating is a bit like booing the ugly sisters in the Christmas pantomime; it will always happen. When it's funny, fair enough, when it's predictable it's boring, and when it gets extremely personal it's bang out of order. Those who shout abuse about players' and refs' wives and families? Well, they really are wankers!

Jeff Winter
February 2010

INTRODUCTION

It's a bright spring morning in 2009 as hordes of Manchester United fans descend on Old Trafford, ready for a battle on – and off – the pitch with arch-rivals Liverpool. Expectant supporters shuffle past the glut of burger vans and horse manure as the big kick-off approaches. There is nothing quite like walking among a sea of strangers, all united in a shared and overwhelming passion for following your team.

Passion can be expressed in a variety of ways. While our long-suffering other halves yearn for a little more attention, one commitment we can all manage is the chance to travel the length and breadth of the country in order to follow our heroes.

And who wants to spend Saturdays window-shopping with 'er indoors when we can hail hard-working midfielders from South Korea?

Park, Park, wherever you may be
You eat dogs in your own country!
It could be worse, you could be Scouse!
Eating rats in your council house!

The tuneful United fans love to sing this heart-warming take on 'Lord of the Dance' whenever their rivals up the East Lancs Road descend on Sir Matt Busby Way. In this instance, however, Liverpool had the last laugh, as they beat their bitter rivals 4–1 at Old Trafford. All of a sudden, with United's supporters stunned into silence, the stadium rang with Liverpool fans' tongue-in-cheek chant:

Rafa's cracking up! He's cracking up!
He's cracking up! He's cracking!
Rafa's cracking up!

Liverpool manager Benitez had become a laughing stock with his infamous 'Fact' rant in January 2009, leading the United supporters to adapt England's Euro '96 anthem 'Three Lions', with its 'Football's Coming Home' chant, to voice their opinion that the Spaniard had lost it. But football has a habit of leaving you disappointed, and when Benitez's men thumped United in March 2009 at Old Trafford, it gave the Merseysiders the chance to bask in the glory of a resounding victory, and they made sure they let everyone know about it.

Political correctness is not something you would associate with us football fans, with our quick wit capable of raising a laugh or two on match-days. Dog is considered a delicacy in Park Ji-Sung's home country, South Korea, and the subject of food often provides supporters with a rich array of humorous anecdotes to belt out from the stands.

Scotland, a country famed for deep-frying just about anything, may lack the credentials to be a powerful footballing force on the pitch, but the Tartan Army are up there with the best of them when it comes to supporting their team. Witness the 'We're gonna deep fry your frogs' legs' chant, sung when the Scots played France in a Euro 2008 qualifier. Absolutely cracking stuff, and another example of when football fans unite for the greater good and give us all a laugh.

Football provides us with an opportunity to put down our rivals, eulogise about the new defensive sensation from Suriname and, in the case of Chelsea supporters, let everyone know about their slightly erotic fixation with celery. It's a question of expression, whether you're sitting in Rushden's Nene Park singing 'Knight Fever' or standing in the Kop belting out 'You'll Never Walk Alone', we all love a good sing-song, never more so than when our tunes get right up our rival fans' noses.

Throughout this book you will find a collection of the funniest and weirdest football chants, from the

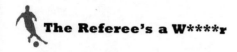

'Hero Worship' section right up to 'Doing the 92', featuring chants from every club in the English Football League. And if you still want more, scoot on over to 'Extra Time', which features a tribute to the late, great, Sir Bobby Robson, along with some cracking quotes from seasons gone by.

Unfortunately, our hatred for our opponents can, occasionally, just get a little out of hand, and we'll be examining the nastier side of football in the 'X-Rated' section of the book. Sometimes fans cross the line, and we'll be trying to understand why they do. However, although some of the darker chants give the majority of football supporters a bad name, we should not all be tarred with the same brush – most of us just want to enjoy a good game of football (which is often easier said than done, depending on what team you support...) and indulge in some light-hearted banter.

So sit back, clear your throat and get ready to belt out all the hits from yesteryear right up to the present day.

And just remember: the referee's a wanker.

CHAPTER ONE:
OLDIES BUT GOODIES

While the five-minute-long serenades to stars past and present may fire our hearts on the terraces, you can't beat pure, classic, comedy gold. Yes, there are the twisted takes on Andrew Lloyd-Webber hits or tributes to Wham!, but often the best songs are the simple classics that have been knocking around for years.

The unwritten rule of an effective football chant is to keep it simple. You don't want to be scratching around for a club's hymn book or nagging those around you with constant requests for lyrics, so, for the casual football fan, 'Oldies But Goodies' does the trick.

Only in the mad, mad world of following your team could such incredible songs spring up and pass the test of time, including a brilliant put-down that name-drops a village in Wales. 'Why's that so

special?' you ask? Well, the village in question has 58 letters in its name!

Each club, be it non-league or Champions League, has its own unique chants but when the time is right, fans right across the world will indulge in some Oldie But Goodie love…

⚽ 'YOU'RE NOT SINGING ANYMORE'

There are few worse feelings than watching your team go behind having taken the lead. The agony, the despair, the sense of 'why didn't you close him down, you ****!'… and, of course, rival supporters love to put the boot in with the most simple of put-downs:

You're not singing anymore!
You're not singing!
You're not singing!
YOU'RE NOT SINGING ANYMORE!

[Sung to the tune of 'Cwm Rhondda', or 'Bread of Heaven', a hymn written by John Hughes. Variations on this include 'Shall we sing a song for you?' and 'It's all gone quiet over there'.]

You would think this wouldn't leave much room for a comeback but, memorably, Fulham fans had the last laugh when they responded to such a chant from Portsmouth fans in 2007. Benjani had scored the opening goal for Pompey in a Premier League game at Craven Cottage – cue a rendition of 'You're not singing'. Fulham's response?

WE WEREN'T SINGING ANYWAY!

[Fulham fans didn't have much to sing about in the end. They ended up losing the match 2–0.]

⚽ CONTINUING THE THEME...

...here are some more ways of appreciating 'Bread of Heaven':

Can we play you every week?

Are you [insert despised team] in disguise?

[Generally sung when your team are winning comfortably. Wrexham fans took this one to a whole new level when they went 5–0 up against Cambridge in 2002. The Welshmen sang: 'Are you Llanfairpwllgwyngyllgogerychwyrndrobwllllantysili ogogogoch in disguise?'! And yes, that IS a real place. It's a small village in Anglesey, Wales.]

Does your butler know you're here?

[Good stuff from West Ham here, taunting the

Cottagers about where they're from. Fulham is a rather affluent area in west London, especially compared to West Ham...]

We can see you washing up!

[Sung by all and sundry while at Leyton Orient's Brisbane Road ground. There are flats situated in the corners of the stadium.]

You're the only one at home!

[More Brisbane Road comedy here. During a Carling Cup tie at home to Stoke, a lone man watched the action from his balcony. Around 2,500 people made sure he had some company.]

You're not ringing anymore!

[Sung by Arsenal fans to John Portsmouth Football Club Westwood (yes, that's his real name), who annoys fans up and down the country with his loud handbell. The Gunners were right; the avid Pompey fan was a little muted when Arsène Wenger's men went 4–1 up in August 2009.]

You're not signing anymore!

[No, that's not a typo – Stoke City fans came up

with this gem when Chelsea visited the Britannia Stadium in September 2009. Following alleged irregularities, UEFA banned Chelsea from transfer activity for two years.]

⚽ 'WHO ATE ALL THE PIES?'

Football fatties have long had to take abuse from fans on one of their many chins. Leading the way in the long list of lardy tributes is an all-time classic:

Who ate all the pies?
Who ate all the pies?
You fat bastard! You fat bastard!
You ate all the pies!

[Sung to the tune of 'Knees up Mother Brown', a 1930s hit by Harris Weston and Bert Lee.]

This classic is one of the milder songs sung by West Ham fans to hate-figure 'Fat' Frank Lampard following his defection to Chelsea in 2001. Fellow victims of the classic include roly-poly Swedish striker Thomas Brolin, whose Michelin-man body graced the Premier League in the 1990s with Leeds and Crystal Palace.

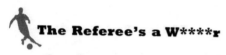

⚽ 'WALKING IN A ... WONDERLAND'

Not all of the classics take the mickey. This delightful ditty is usually reserved for players and/or managers to have played and/or managed their way into the hearts of the supporters. Scoring twice against your hated rivals helps, as does winning trophies.

There's only one Arsène Wenger!
One Arsène Wenger!
Walking along, singing a song
Walking in a Wenger wonderland!

[Sung to the tune of 'Winter Wonderland', a song penned in the 1930s by Felix Bernard. It's been covered by everyone from Ozzy Osbourne to Dolly Parton to Frank Sinatra. Strangely enough, the ode to Wenger has died down slightly following Arsenal's lengthy run without a trophy.]

There's only one Carlton Palmer!
And he smokes marijuana!
He's six foot tall and his head's too small
Walking in a Palmer wonderland!

[An excellent use of the 'Winter Wonderland' tune, sung by Sheffield Wednesday fans in the 1990s. The Wednesday fans didn't literally mean Palmer liked the odd jazzy cigarette – they used the line because it rhymed. Just like that.]

There's only one Emile Heskey!
One Emile Heskey!
He used to be shite
But now he's alright
Walking in a Heskey wonderland!

[Sung about much-maligned striker Emile Heskey. Started by Wigan and inherited by Aston Villa following Heskey's arrival in 2009.]

⚽ 'BY FAR THE GREATEST TEAM'

Strange one, this. On the one hand, bellowing out the assertion that your team is the greatest in the world can be a rousing way of announcing your dominance. On the other hand, it's sung by Huddersfield fans and the like.

And it's Huddersfield!
Huddersfield FC! We're by far the greatest team!
The world has ever seen!

[Every club sings this one, hence its inclusion in the 'Oldies But Goodies' list. The chant is usually heard at grounds where the fans' repertoire of witty songs is a little sparse.]

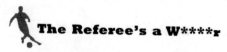

⚽ 'YOU'RE SHIT, AND YOU KNOW YOU ARE'

Following on from Huddersfield fans claiming their team are world-beaters, the typical response from terrace rivals is a put-down to silence the optimistic crowd:

You're shit, and you know you are! [repeat]

[To the tune of 'Go West', by the Pet Shop Boys. Variations on a similar theme include 'Can we play you every week?', which is usually sung when a team races into a commanding lead inside the first half.]

You're shish and you know you are!
You're shish and you know you are!
You're shish and you know you are!
You're shish and you know you are!

[Excellent work from Chelsea supporters, who belted this one out to Galatasaray during a Champions League clash in 1999.]

⚽ 'QUE SERA, SERA'

We can't have a list of classics without this one. Usually reserved for the FA Cup, fans sing it to remind their downbeat rivals which of the two teams on the pitch is going off to the final at Wembley.

Que Sera, Sera
Whatever will be, will be
We're going to Wem-ber-ley!
Que Sera! Sera!

[To the tune of 'Que Sera, Sera', a 1950s song written by Jay Livingston and Ray Evans. Manchester United fans replaced 'Wem-ber-ley' with 'I-ta-ly' while crowing about their impending trip to Rome for the 2009 Champions League final. Bet they wish they hadn't gone there now...]

⚽ 'DO-DO-DO-DO'

The Middlesbrough players run out to this catchy disco hit from the 1990s and the dance-floor smash has made its way into other grounds across the country. It's plain, simple and popular, making it worthy of classic status.

Do-do-do-do!
Andy Johnson!
Do-do-do-do!
Andy Johnson!

[To the tune of the Perfecto Allstars' 'Reach Up (Papa's Got A Brand New Pigbag)'.]

 The Referee's a W****r

⚽ 'WE SHALL NOT BE MOVED'

Picture the scene. There's one minute left of injury time and you REALLY need your £30 million man to stick one in the back of the net – otherwise you're kissing your title dreams goodbye. Then – BANG! He smashes one in from two yards and you're top of the table going into the final day…

We shall not, we shall not be moved!
We shall not, we shall not be moved!
Just like the team that's gonna win the Football League (again!)
We shall not be moved!

⚽ 'E-I-E-I-O'

No, nothing to do with some old bloke and a farm. This is a rather new one that sprung up around Football League grounds in the 2008/09 season. First heard at Leicester City's Walkers Stadium as early as September 2008, Foxes fans were optimistic about their team's chances of getting promoted. How right they were.

E-i-e-i-e-i-o! Up the Football League we go!
When we get promotion
This is what we'll sing:
'We are champions!'

'We are champions!'
Nigel Pearson's king!

[This clearly caught on and was heard up and down the country throughout the season, so just replace Nigel Pearson's name with the name of your club's manager.]

⚽ 'GUANTANAMERA'

As you will come to realise, 'Guantanamera' provides the basis for a whole raft of supporters' songs. The tune's roots are based in Cuba and, strangely, the song is about a man's love for a steak sandwich-making woman. The beauty in this tune is that each tribute is never longer than two lines, making it instantly recognisable among those in the stands.

Score in a brothel! You couldn't score in a brothel!
Score in a brothel! You couldn't score in a brothel!

[We've all been there. No, not a brothel – on the terraces when a serial opportunity-squanderer misses the target once again. Victims in the past include Diego Forlan, Ade Akinbiyi, Didier Drogba (before he turned decent), Peter Crouch and many more.]

Small town in... [insert name of hated village/town/city/county/country here]

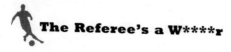

The Referee's a W****r

You're just a small town in...
Small town in...
You're just a small town in...

[Typical chant taunting a club's stature. Arsenal fans sing 'You're just a small town in Fulham' to Chelsea supporters.]

One [insert player name...]
There's only one...
One...
There's only one...

[General admiration for a player. A quick glance at the electoral register would prove most supporters wrong when they sing this, but we get the point. Hull fans brilliantly sang 'One Gordon Ramsay' at Norwich in 2006 as they mocked Canaries supremo and top chef Delia Smith.]

Live round the corner!
You only live round the corner!
Live round the corner!
You only live round the corner!

[Mainly sung to Manchester United fans when they are at an away match in London. The song plays on the stereotype that half the United supporters in the country live in London and only started following

the team when they started to become successful in
the early 1990s.]

Down in a minute!
We're going down in a minute!
Down in a minute!
We're going down in a minute!

[Gallows humour from fans witnessing their team
on the verge of relegation.]

Gone Christmas shopping!
You should've gone Christmas shopping!
Gone Christmas shopping!
You should've gone Christmas shopping!

[Festive fixture going to plan? Sing this to your
rival supporters.]

Juan Pablo Angel!
There's only Juan Pablo Angel!

[Well done, Aston Villa. Great word-play from
the Villains, saluting Columbian striker Juan
Pablo Angel.]

Sing when you're winning!
You only sing when you're winning!

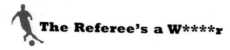

The Referee's a W****r

[A sly dig at fair-weather football fans who only seem to become vocal when their team is doing well. During a World Cup qualifier in 2008, Scotland supporters sang 'You only sing when you're whaling' to Norway!]

⚽ WHILE WE'RE ON THE SUBJECT OF SINGING...

When your team's 3–0 down, it is more difficult than usual to belt out your favourite terrace tunes with the same fervour as you would if the scoreline was reversed. And, of course, it takes mere seconds for rival fans to sense your growing discomfort. We've all been there:

Can you hear the [team] sing? [Whoa! Whoa!]
Can you hear the [team] sing? [Whoa! Whoa!]
Can you hear the [team] sing?
I can't hear a fucking thing!
Whoa!

⚽ MY GARDEN SHED

It can be a traumatic experience standing in the away end at Brighton's Withdean Stadium. The stadium – the term is used loosely – is the Seagulls' temporary home until they move to their state-of-the-art ground in Falmer.

The away 'stand' is about 20 yards away from the

pitch and the stadium itself can hardly be described as expansive. So the following chant gets a fair few minutes of airtime at the Withdean and it also crops up across the country whenever fans visit stadiums that are a little on the small side:

My garden shed! (My garden shed!)
Is bigger than this! (Is bigger than this!)
My garden shed is bigger than this!
It's got a door and a window!
My garden shed is bigger than this!

[To the tune of 'When The Saints Go Marching In'.]

⚽ CONTINUING THE TUNE...

Football fans are always eager to proclaim their hometown to be the best, which is why this chant earns its inclusion in the list. Feminists look away now... plenty of teams sing this one, but we're using West Ham as a typical example:

Oh east London! (Oh east London!)
Is wonderful! (Is wonderful!)
Oh east London is won-der-ful...
It's full of tits, fanny and West Ham!
Oh east London is won-der-ful!

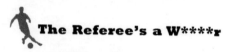

⚽ HEY JUDE

As you can see, simplicity and rhythm are key for a chant to work. And you can't get simpler than this take on the Beatles' 'Hey Jude'. The end word of the song can be the name of your town, club or your favourite footballer – whatever fits. So:

Na na na na na na na, na na na na... The Gills!

[The Gills refers to Gillingham.]

⚽ 'GIVE US A WAVE'

Nice one, this. Usually sung by jubilant supporters at their manager, with the team coasting. With everything going to plan on the pitch, the fans sing:

Fergie,* give us a wave!
Fergie, Fergie give us a wave!

*Or whoever. If the manager obliges, massive choruses of cheers spring up to salute the boss for doing as requested.

This can be adapted to form a sly dig at the opposition when your team are winning:

Rafa, what's the score?

20

Rafa, Rafa, what's the score!

Leeds took this chant to another level when they were trouncing Tranmere 3–0 in August 2009, with a great put-down aimed at John Barnes:

Barnesy, give us a rap!
Barnesy, Barnesy, give us a rap!

[Barnesy loves a good rap – from his contribution to New Order's excellent 1990 World Cup anthem 'World in Motion' to the frankly quite bizarre 'Anfield Rap', he's got those rhymes down!]

Norwich fans sang this one to their own player, Cody McDonald, after he came on as a substitute against Sunderland in the Carling Cup:

Cody, touch the bar!
Cody, Cody, touch the bar!

[Little Cody couldn't oblige, perhaps because he's only 5ft 7in...]

Bolton fans have adopted a brilliant-but-harsh variation on this song. It's no secret that Trotters fans despise their own manager, Gary Megson, despite the carrot-topped maestro keeping his team in the Premier League in both seasons since his

appointment, as well as drawing with Bayern Munich away in the UEFA Cup in 2007.

Bless him, he's just not liked that much at the Reebok. And the feeling towards Megson was hilariously summed up during Bolton's home clash against Stoke City in October 2009 with:

Bolton fans:

Megson, give us a wave!
Megson, Megson give us a wave!

[Megson waves]

Bolton fans respond:

Who are ya? Who are ya?

Megson's face was a picture!

⚽ BEST OF THE REST

United! United!

[Rallying cry for teams called United. Usually provokes a reaction of 'ARE SHIT! ARE SHIT!' from rival fans.]

Stand up if you love [team]

['Go West' provides the inspiration again here. The song's popularity rose dramatically after all-seater stadiums were introduced. Nostalgic fans are reminded of the good old days of terracing, while everyone else gets a great opportunity to irritate the stewards, who invariably want everyone to remain seated. Win-win situation. Also, fans of the reigning Premier League champions sing 'Stand up for the champions' to show their support.]

How wide do you want the goal?
How wide do you want the goal?

[Has the same meaning as the 'Score in a brothel' chant.]

What-a waste-a money!

[Striker with a measly goal return? Sing this snappy number.]

Dirty northern bastards!

[Southern fans sing this to antagonise their northern rivals. Plymouth Argyle supporters sing it to anyone!]

Who are ya? Who are ya? Who are ya?

The Referee's a W****r

[Sung whenever an obscure name comes on to the pitch, or when a lower-league team taunts their more illustrious opposition after taking the lead. Think Barnsley when they went 1–0 up in their FA Cup sixth-round clash against Chelsea in 2008.]

Sit down, shut up, sit down, shut up!

[Nice and simple – a traditional terrace taunt for those who angrily question a referee's decision. If the fans are screaming for a penalty and don't get it, rival supporters sing 'sit down, shut up' to compound the misery.]

The Great Escape

[The theme tune to the film 'The Great Escape' provides fans with a tuneful and rhythmic way of humming your team's name. It is usually sung by supporters of relegation-threatened clubs, who urge their team to pull off their very own great escape by avoiding the drop.]

Now you've limbered up with some good old classics, it's time to tackle the 'Funnies'…

CHAPTER TWO:
FUNNIES

Football fans are blessed with a sharp wit and, when the creative juices are flowing, the results can be spectacular. Who needs to go and pay £40 to watch a comedian in the West End when you can pay a few quid to witness Dorchester Town's take on Toni Basil's 'Hey Mickey'?

Up and down the country we have seen some hilarious, quick-fire reactions to action on the pitch and in this section you will unearth some comedy gems – keep your eyes peeled for a cracker from a pre-season match between Chesterfield and Partick Thistle.

⚽ IT'S A COMPETITIVE FIELD, BUT...

...the chant for Andy Goram – who was diagnosed with schizophrenia towards the end of his career –

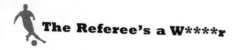

is a leading contender for funniest football chant, even if it is just a little cruel. When the Rangers goalkeeper stepped on to the field for the first time since his condition was made public, it didn't take long for this cracking chorus to spring up:

Two Andy Gorams!
There's only two Andy Gorams!

[To the tune of, you've guessed it, 'Guantanamera'.]

Absolute belter.

⚽ TWO KERRYS

In the same vein...

Two Kerry Mayos!
There's only two Kerry Mayos!

[Brighton fans loved to sing this about defender Kerry Mayo – whose wife is also called Kerry.]

⚽ WITH LOVE FROM ACROSS THE POND...

American soccerball fans thought it was totally wicked awesome when David Beckham came over to play for the LA Galaxy in 2007, but clearly wife Victoria hadn't made the best impression prior to

her arrival in Tinseltown.

We sing better than your wife!

[To the tune of 'Bread of Heaven' and heard as early as Beckham's debut on 9 August 2007 against DC United.]

⚽ 'YOU DO THE CRISTIANO'

Cristiano Ronaldo used to be idolised at Old Trafford, but the Portuguese playmaker angered Manchester United fans when he openly pined for a move to Real Madrid following United's Champions League final victory in 2008. A year later he got his wish and, despite enjoying six trophy-laden years at United, some of the fans were rather miffed at his decision to leave.

Although the following song hasn't been sung with quite as much gusto as past Old Trafford hits, it has caught on and has also been heard doing the rounds among fans of the other clubs in the 'Big Four':

You put your transfer in, your transfer out,
In out, in out, you fuck your club about,
You do the Cristiano and you change your mind,
That's what it's all about!
Oh, Ronaldo is a wanker! Oh, Ronaldo is a wanker!
Oh, Ronaldo is a wanker...

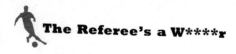

Knees bent, arms stretched, DIVE! DIVE! DIVE!

[To the tune of the 'Hokey Cokey'.]

⚽ 'VIVA JOHN TERRY'

As you can see, United fans' appreciation for Cristiano Ronaldo has dwindled somewhat. Perhaps saying he wanted to leave the club a couple of weeks after winning the Champions League was not the best idea. While the masses in Manchester used to sing 'Viva Ronaldo', the song died out during the 2008/09 season and a new variation sprung up, commemorating the penalty shoot-out cock-up from Chelsea captain John Terry.

If he had scored in the shoot-out in Moscow, Chelsea would have won the 2008 Champions League final, but he slipped and booted the ball – and Chelsea's hopes – against the post. United went on to win, and didn't their fans love it:

Viva John Terry! Viva John Terry!
Could've won the cup!
But he fucked it up!
Viva John Terry!

⚽ 'BOOGIE'

Emmanuel Eboue has a bit of a boos problem at

Arsenal. In a match against Wigan in December 2008, the poor Ivorian defender was substituted for his own good by manager Arsène Wenger. Eboue was having a nightmare at the Emirates – constantly giving the ball away, mistiming tackles and getting in the way of his own team-mates. The Gunners fans were sick and tired of his inept display and booed his every touch, prompting Wenger to do the honourable thing and haul Eboue off before things really turned bad.

At least Eboue's team-mate Kolo Toure had some nice words for him, saying: 'The fans gave him a hard time and that is not usual at Arsenal. He has all our support because we know he is a great player. He tries his best for the team, even if he is not 100 per cent ready. I was surprised, because normally our fans are nice always. I think the tension was really high and that is why they were hard.'

Eboue would be well advised to listen to Toure, especially considering the (quite excellent, it must be said) song the Arsenal fans sing about their much-maligned defender:

Don't blame it on the Henry
Don't blame it on the injuries
Don't blame it on the referee
Blame it on Eboue!

[To the tune of 'Blame It on the Boogie', by the

Jackson Five. The Arsenal fans are a tough bunch, but they do spare Eboue the embarrassment of hearing this song *every* time he plays. The Jackson Five tribute usually only does the rounds when Wenger's men are enduring a difficult spell.]

Liverpool brilliantly adapted the 'Boogie' song in 2005 after watching Djimi Traore score a comical own goal during an FA Cup third round clash against Burnley. The defender executed a stunning, Zinedine Zidane-esque flick that sailed past the goalkeeper – just too bad it was Liverpool goalkeeper Jerzy Dudek. The goal was enough to stun the Merseysiders and knock them out of the cup. YouTube it, you won't be disappointed. In the meantime:

Don't blame it on the Hamann
Don't blame it on the Biscan
Don't blame it on the Finnan
Blame it on Traore!
He just can't, he just can't, he just can't control his feet!

⚽ 'I'M 'AVIN' THAT'

Garry Flitcroft, the former Manchester City and Blackburn Rovers midfielder, once fought a year-long battle to stop the *Sunday People* from revealing

Funnies

sordid details about his personal life. In 2002, the gagging order was lifted and the full extent of Flitcroft's fun was revealed. The married father-of-two had been exposed as a 'love rat', but, unlike Mrs Flitcroft, at least the Blackburn fans loved him:

Garry Flitcroft's magic
He wears a magic hat
And when he saw that lap dancer
He said 'I'm shagging that'!

[To the tune of 'My Old Man's a Dustman'.]

⚽ 'HEY NICKY'

Nick Eyre made his debut for St Albans in August 2007, but couldn't stop Dorchester Town from romping to a 3–0 win. The Town fans were a clever bunch and, after realising Eyre was making his bow, they quickly came up with a brilliant way to humiliate him following a goal from Hardy Pinto-Moreira:

Hey Nicky, you're so fine
You're so fine you're two behind
Hey Nicky! Hey, hey, hey Nicky!

[To the tune of 'Hey Mickey', by Toni Basil.]

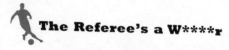

⚽ HERE'S LOOKING AT YOU, KID

Football fans can be a cruel bunch – just ask Jason Lee, who makes an appearance in the 'Heroes' section. Lee's pineapple-style haircut caused him much grief during his playing career, but the former Nottingham Forest striker can seek consolation in the fact his fellow professionals didn't escape terrace humour when it was deserved.

Get your 'Guantanamera' hats on for:

You're just a fat Eddie Murphy!

[Fans of multiple Championship clubs sang this one to Cardiff striker Jimmy Floyd Hasselbaink while he was a Bluebird. The former Chelsea man bears more than a passing resemblance to the *Dr Dolittle* star – and good-humoured Hasselbaink deserves praise for laughing at the chant directed at him. Paul Ince got the same treatment when he took his Blackburn Rovers side to West Ham in 2008, as did Jean-Claude Darcheville, when he played for Rangers.]

You're just a fat Paris Hilton!

[You would expect to read about opposition fans taunting Liverpool striker Andriy Voronin, but this chant did the rounds in the Kop during his ill-fated

stay on Merseyside. Clearly riled by his meagre goal return, the Kopites turned on the striker and he was subsequently loaned out to German giants Hertha Berlin, before he rejoined the club again in time for the start of the 2008/09 season.]

You're just a fat Kevin Doyle!

[Wolves fans remind Robbie Keane there's only one Republic of Ireland hitman worth the entrance fee.]

There's only one Tina Turner!

[Nottingham Forest fans, clearly forgetting their association with our friend Mr Lee, castigate Doncaster's Jason Price for his extravagant hairstyle.]

You're just a thin Whoopi Goldberg!

[Superb put-down directed towards Frank Sinclair. The midfielder, who went on to star for England in the 2002 World Cup, sported some fetching dreadlocks during his early days and the response from the terraces was predictable.]

There's only one David Gower!

[During a Premier League match between Leeds and West Ham in 2002, David James was given a great

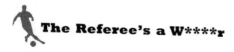

welcome when he took to the field sporting his new curly blonde bonce.]

There's only one Roland Browning!

[More gems from the non-league here. Eastleigh substitute Steve Watts was likened to chubby *Grange Hill* student Browning during a match against Bognor in the 2008/09 season.]

You're just a fat Spanish waiter!

[Manchester United supporters love to goad Rafael Benitez with this sing-song about the Spaniard's appearance.]

There's only one Alan Rickman!

[Wigan fans had little reason to smile when they lost 5–0 to Manchester United in August 2009 – but they cheered themselves up with this chant for Dimitar Berbatov, who bears an uncanny resemblance to Rickman's character in the *Harry Potter* films, Professor Snape.]

Get ready to sing to the tune of 'He's here, he's there, he's every-fucking-where' for this tribute to jug-eared Sheffield Wednesday striker Francis Jeffers, courtesy of the Owls' fans themselves:

He's big, he's Scouse
He looks like Mickey Mouse!
Franny-J! Franny-J!

And it's 'Bread of Heaven' for Leeds United's hilarious tribute to David Prutton:

You're not Jesus anymore!

[This was sung in response to Prutton's change of appearance. He used to sport a Jesus-esque hairdo and facial hair, but adopted a more clean-cut look for the 2009/10 season.]

⚽ 'NEVILLE NEVILLE'

The father of Gary and Phil Neville is called... Neville Neville. Seriously. Hence the quite genius:

Neville Neville, they're in defence
Neville Neville, their future's immense
Neville Neville, like Jacko they're bad
Neville Neville, the name of their dad!

[To the tune of 'Rebel Rebel', by David Bowie.]

Nothing can top that song, but while we're on the subject of the Neville family, here are two great titbits from the clan, starting with Gary on David

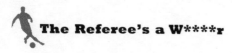

Beckham's marriage to Spice Girl Victoria:

'I was with David that fateful night he first saw the Spice Girls on the telly and said, "See that girl who can't dance or sing? I'm going to marry her."' Priceless!

And now on to Neville Neville himself, from a newspaper report covering a pre-World Cup 2006 party, attended by the England team and their WAGs:

'Then Neville Neville, father of England defender Gary Neville, stood on a couch to lead the WAGs in a version of the National Anthem as they smashed champagne glasses on a table...'

You would think with all their cash, cars and bling, the modern-day footballer and his missus would be above the raucous singing and hero-worship everyday fans indulge in. Not one bit.

From the same report:

'Fuelled by bottles of Moët champagne drunk with strawberry syrup, glasses of vodka, Red Bull and shots of Sambucca, they ignored the techno music on offer to start their own sing-song, beginning with: "We're not going home, we're not going home."

Next came a singing competition about their partners. Coleen screamed out: "Rooney,

Rooney!"; Elen Rives chanted: "Super Frank, super Frankie Lampard!"; Lisa Roughead shouted: "There's only one Michael Carrick!"; and Michaela Henderson-Thynne sang: "There's only one Stewart Downing!"'

Elen Rives may have been very vocal in her support for fiancé Frank at that party in Baden-Baden in 2006, but, following their acrimonious split three years later, she'd probably prefer to join in with a chorus of:

Ten men went to lift
Went to lift Frank Lampard
Ten men and their forklift truck
Went to lift Frank Lampard!

[Sung to the tune of 'One Man Went to Mow', a terrace favourite at Stamford Bridge. Many fans like this one, but the most vocal anti-Lampard chants are reserved for West Ham followers, who are still incensed by the England midfielder's defection to Chelsea in 2001.]

⚽ 'IT'LL END IN TEARS'

Manchester City were the subject of much derision following their botched attempt to sign AC Milan star Kaka in 2009, and the Brazilian's decision to

snub their millions inspired this amusing chant from those in the red half of Manchester:

Kaka, wherever you may be
Have you heard of Man City?
Don't go there, it'll end in tears
They've not won a trophy in 30 years!

[To the tune of popular hymn 'Lord of the Dance'.]

Time for more inter-city rivalry and a great line from Fulham concerning Chelsea's controversial Champions League semi-final exit to Barcelona in 2009.

In a nutshell, referee Tom Henning Ovrebo had a stinker; a real, real stinker. He failed to give Chelsea what looked like four clear penalties and received death threats from fans outraged by his shocking performance.

This seemingly blatant disregard for the Laws of the Game (see Gerard Piqué's handball in the Chelsea penalty area) led some conspiracy theorists to suggest that Henning was under orders from UEFA president Michel Platini to stop a second consecutive all-English Champions League final, following the Manchester United–Chelsea clash in Moscow in 2008.

So, over to Fulham:

Chelsea, whoever you may be
You've been done by a con-spir-a-cy
Barca drew, so they go through
To a final wanted by Pla-ti-ni

[To the tune of 'Lord of the Dance', again.]

⚽ WOOLIES

Scottish side Hearts have struggled financially for many a year and, as their off-the-pitch wobbles continued during the 2008/09 campaign, Hibernian used a contemporary example to highlight the plight of their Edinburgh rivals:

Are you Woolworths in disguise?

[To the tune of 'Bread of Heaven'.]

⚽ 'SUMMER HOLIDAY'

Continuing the theme of mocking a team's financial woes, here's Arsenal fans' contribution to the genre at the Emirates in late January 2009:

You're not going on a summer holiday!
A summer holiday, a summer holiday!

[To the tune of 'Yellow Submarine', by The Beatles.

The song was in response to the collapse of West Ham's sponsors, the airline XL.]

⚽ 'WE PAY YOUR SPONSORSHIP'

Arsenal fans again on the financially-themed offensive, this time laughing at Newcastle supporters around the time when the Magpies' sponsor, Northern Rock, went bust. The government bailed out the troubled bank, which meant chants about Newcastle's beleaguered sponsors were quick to spring up:

We pay your sponsorship, we pay your sponsorship!

[To the tune of Giuseppe Verdi's opera 'Rigoletto'.]

⚽ 'YOUR CAR'S TOO FAST FOR YOU'

Another example of fans' ability to rapidly concoct a contemporary put-down after hearing some damning news about a high-profile player:

Your car's too fast for you!

[To the tune of Giuseppe Verdi's opera 'Rigoletto' and sung by Derby County fans during an FA Cup clash with Manchester United in 2009. Cristiano Ronaldo played at Pride Park and the home fans

were quick to laugh about him crashing his Ferrari in a tunnel on the way to training in the run-up to the match.]

⚽ 'YOU AIN'T GOT NO HISTORY'

When Chelsea won the league title for the first time in 50 years in 2005, we all thought a shift of power was about to take place. Jose Mourinho's side then retained their Premier League crown, before they lost their grip on the title. Those outside Stamford Bridge loved seeing the rich Londoners struggle to win the league and, woeful grammar and unfounded allegations aside, this song has become popular:

Chelsea, wherever you may be
You ain't got no history
Frank Lampard's fat
Joe Cole's queer
You're gonna win fuck-all this year!

[To the tune of 'Carefree', the Chelsea anthem.]

⚽ 'SHALL WE POACH AN EGG FOR YOU?'

Poor old Kirk Broadfoot was once left with egg on his face – literally – when two eggs he had poached in the microwave exploded, squirting scalding water on to the Rangers defender.

Rangers manager Walter Smith said at the time: 'He's got some facial burns, but he should be okay.' Kirk did indeed make a full recovery from his assault-by-egg and during a match against Aberdeen, he was made, through the medium of 'Bread of Heaven', aware of the Dons fans' desire to give him a hand in the kitchen:

Shall we poach an egg for you?

⚽ 'DEEP FRY YOUR PIZZA'

The Scots, famed for their deep-fried Mars bars, make yet another appearance in the list with their hilarious warning to Italian fans during a Euro 2008 qualifier in November 2007. Once again, 'Guantanamera' is the tune:

We're gonna deep fry your pizzas!

Rangers supporters have taken this superb line one step further and, despite having no regard for simple physics, they warned fans of Russian side Zenit St Petersburg they would deep fry their vodka during the UEFA Cup final in 2008!

The Tartan Army deserve a round of applause for their supreme wit, despite their national team's continued struggles on the pitch. If ever there was a World Cup for chanting, they would definitely

get past the group stage. Just have a look at these:

It's just a big fucking pylon!

['Guantanamera', directed towards France fans and referring to the Eiffel Tower.]

What the hell is va-va-voom?

[More mickey-taking towards the French, this time focusing on Thierry Henry and those Renault Clio ads. 'Bread of Heaven' is the tune.]

While deep-fried pizzas and fucking big pylons make fantastic song material, an absent Baltic football team and dodgy floodlights provides us with a cracking chorus from 1996.

Scotland were due to play Estonia in a World Cup qualifier, but, after a disagreement about floodlights, the match was moved to 3pm so they wouldn't have to be used.

Estonia were furious and refused to turn up for the fixture. This resulted in a remarkable 'match' that lasted three seconds. Scotland kicked off, despite the fact there was no team to play! The game was swiftly abandoned and, amid the farce, the Tartan Army provided us with a memorable (and correct) version of events:

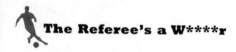

The Referee's a W****r

One team in Tallinn!
There's only one team in Tallinn!

[To the tune of 'Guantanamera'.]

For the record, Scotland didn't fare too well in the re-arranged game, drawing 0–0 with the minnows. They eventually managed to qualify for World Cup in 1998, but were knocked out of the competition and were back at home before the postcards had left the French sorting office.

⚽ 'WANKY WEST HAM'

You put your Argies in, took your Argies out
The Iceman comes and your manager's out
You're selling Reo-Coker and you're going down
That's why we like to shout:
Oh, wanky wanky West Ham!
Oh, wanky wanky West Ham!
Oh, wanky wanky West Ham!
That's what it's all about!

[To the tune of the 'Hokey Cokey'. This song perfectly sums up West Ham's season in 2006/07 – the arrival of Argentine duo Javier Mascherano and Carlos Tevez, the sacking of manager Alan Pardew, the departures of Reo-Coker, Mascherano and Tevez and the buy-out by Icelandic businessman Eggert

Magnusson. The only factual inaccuracy is that they actually survived relegation on the last day of the season. Still, seven out of eight ain't bad, and it's a great song to boot.]

⚽ 'COS MAYBE...'

World Cup-winner Alan Ball endured a difficult, and controversial, spell as Manchester City manager between 1995 and 1996. City were relegated during his tenure and financial constraints meant Ball had to sell a string of big-name players.

The City fans were unhappy and ripped off the Oasis hit 'Wonderwall' to show their displeasure:

'Cos maybe
We should have got Liam Brady
But after all
We got Alan Ball!

⚽ 'FOOTBALL IN A LIBRARY'

A home draw against Hull City in 2009 spelled the end of Luiz Felipe Scolari's reign as Chelsea manager. Chelsea went into the match in poor form and the fans were clearly nervous about the future, which explains why Stamford Bridge was very, very quiet.

At least the Tigers fans livened things up with this brilliant variation of 'Agadoo' by Black Lace:

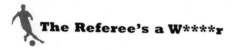

The Referee's a W****r

Agadoo-doo-doo
Push pineapple, shake a tree
Agadoo-doo-doo
Football in a lib-ra-ry!

⚽ TERRACE BATTLES PART ONE...

When Roman Abramovich took over at Chelsea in 2004, he erased their mounting debts and piled millions of pounds into the club. As a result, in a match against Arsenal in 2005, the Blues fans goaded the Gunners – who were struggling to finance their new stadium – with this:

Shall we buy a ground for you?

Arsenal fought back immediately with a well-crafted response:

Shall we win the league for you?

[Both sung to the tune of 'Bread of Heaven'. Chelsea, in fact, didn't need any help with winning the league that year. They finished as champions for the first time in 50 years, while Arsenal finished second, 13 points behind their rich rivals.]

More Abramovich-related takeover talk:

Debt-free, wherever we may be
We're gonna buy everyone we see
And we don't give a fuck about the fee
'Cos we are the wealthy CFC

[To the tune of Chelsea anthem, 'Carefree'. It's the same as 'Lord of the Dance'.]

TERRACE BATTLES PART TWO...

Brighton supporters know a thing or two about homophobic chanting, but most of the time it's just part and parcel of terrace humour. Nothing malicious is meant when fans sing 'Does you boyfriend know you're here?' – it's just light-hearted banter that shouldn't be taken too seriously.

This dual between Watford and Newcastle supporters highlights just how funny it can be when fans bounce chants off each other:

Are you shagging Elton John?

[Newcastle fans to the home supporters in the Carling Cup tie at Watford in 2006.]

Are you shagging Ant 'n' Dec?

[Watford's response.]

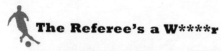

⚽ TERRACE BATTLES PART THREE...

Chelsea's 2–1 victory over Reading in 2006 will always be remembered for Petr Cech's sickening injury. The Czech goalkeeper suffered a shattered skull following a challenge from Stephen Hunt. The Reading star then endured entirely predictable chants of 'Hunt is a c**t', but this great battle on the terraces did lighten up the mood:

You play like QPR!

[Reading to Chelsea fans.]

You look like QPR!

[Chelsea fans respond.]

You're shit like QPR!

[Chelsea land the knockout blow.]

⚽ TERRACE BATTLES NORTH OF THE BORDER...

Celtic reached the final of the UEFA Cup in 2003 and the Bhoys were eager to let their bitter rivals Rangers know about it:

You'll be watching *The Bill* – when we're in Seville

Walking in a Celtic wonderland!

[To the tune of 'Winter Wonderland'.]

Celtic's cup dreams fell flat when they lost 3–2 to Porto, leading the Rangers fans to crow about their demise:

We were watching *The Bill* – what was the score in Seville?

⚽ TERRACE HUMOUR

Terrace humour is great – especially when one set of fans lands a real knockout blow. Live banter between both sets of supporters usually ends in hilarious results and a match between Newcastle and Fulham in the Premier League in 2008 is a great example. Newcastle fans, in the knowledge that their team was comfortably in mid-table, started taunting Fulham with:

Going down, going down, going down!

But Fulham had the last laugh with this excellent reply; one that left the home fans silent:

So are we, so are we, so are we!

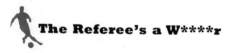

[Fulham actually escaped relegation on the final day of the season, and went on to clinch a place in the 2009/10 Europa League. Newcastle, however, were relegated the following season.]

⚽ IT'S FUNNY 'COS IT'S TRUE...

Tom Hanks is a big Aston Villa fan, although his reason for supporting them remains questionable. He once said: 'I'm big on Aston Villa. The name is so sweet, it sounds like a lovely spa.'

The Villains love having Forrest Gump as a celebrity fan and belt out this simple medley every time he is in town. Which has been once, so far.

Forrest Gump is an Aston Villa fan!
An Aston Villa fan, an Aston Villa fan!

[To the tune of 'Yellow Submarine' by the Beatles.]

⚽ OLDHAM

This is superb:

Give us a T... Give us an I... Give us a T... Give us an S...
What we gonna do?
Oldham! Oldham! Oldham!

⚽ 'SHE'S HERE, SHE'S THERE…'

In 2006, Sheffield United goalkeeper Paddy Kenny was dumped by his wife – for one of his mates. To make matters worse, Kenny was being treated for a hamstring problem when he found out wife Karen had been playing away with a lover. The pair enjoyed a romantic weekend at a hotel, apparently. Here's what a friend of Paddy's told a tabloid newspaper at the time: 'Paddy and Karen were in the process of moving house – so he obviously thought they were making plans, but, in reality she was having an affair with his friend behind his back. It came completely out of the blue, no one had any idea. He is distraught. He really loved Karen and assumed they had a long future together.'

Newcastle United fans, however, had no sympathy for distraught Paddy a week or so after the news broke. The Blades keeper suffered at the hands of the baying Tyneside mob, with chants of:

She's here, she's there
She's every-fucking-where
Paddy's wife! Paddy's wife!

⚽ ON THE SUBJECT OF PLAYING AWAY…

Picture this: it's 1980 and England goalkeeper Peter Shilton is inside his Jaguar with Tina Street, round

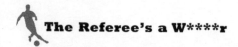

the back of Nottingham racecourse. Tina's husband, Colin, is knocking on the steamy windows of the car, trying to get inside. Colin decides to call the police after failing to gain entry – but Shilts and Street make a break for it and speed off.

The botched getaway ends in disaster as Shilton drives straight into a lamp-post. He admits to 'taking a lady for a meal' and, after failing a breath test, is banned from driving for 15 months. We all had a field day.

Does your missus know you're here?
Does your missus know you're here!

[To the tune of 'Bread of Heaven'.]

Or, simply:

Tina! Tina! Tina!

⚽ LASAGNE

Tottenham were on the verge of pipping Arsenal to the fourth remaining Champions League place in 2006. They went into their match against West Ham on the final day of the season needing a win to have a chance of finishing above the Gunners, but, on the day of the match, half the team was struck down by a mystery virus. Spurs lost 2–1 to the Hammers and

it was suggested – though never proved – that Martin Jol's men had eaten a laxative-laced lasagne before the match, courtesy of an Arsenal fan eager to scupper their chances of finishing fourth! Gunners fans thought all their Christmases had come at once:

Lasagne! Whoa! Lasagne! Whoa!
We laughed ourselves to bits
When Tottenham had the shits!

As a result, Tottenham missed out on a lucrative place in the Champions League and had to settle for a place in the UEFA Cup instead.

It could have been Sky
But it's now Channel Five
That's... lasagne!

[To the tune of 'That's Amore' by Dean Martin. The song reflects the fact that Sky Sports televised Champions League football – while the comparatively low-budget Channel Five had rights to the Champions League's uglier sibling, the UEFA Cup.]

⚽ 'WE FED IT TO PARK'

In May 2007, Chelsea manager Jose Mourinho packed his dog 'Gullit' off to St Tropez to avoid it being sent

into quarantine. Police wanted the Yorkshire terrier because they feared it could have rabies, but a quick-thinking Mourinho beat them to the punch and sent the pooch on an enforced holiday.

The Special One said: 'I told the police officers to wait a little. I went into the house where my children could not stop crying. I sent the dog to St Tropez and I returned 15 minutes later through the main door. What was the reaction of the police when they saw me? They asked me where I'd gone. My reply was "Me, I'm the invisible man".'

The 'Special One' was arrested, but later released, while the police never did get their hands on Gullit. And Mourinho must have been thankful Manchester United fans never found his dog, considering what they sung about him during the 2007 FA Cup final:

Mourinho, are you listening?
Your little dog, it went missing!
It started to bark
So we fed it to Park
Walking in a Fergie wonderland!

[United supporters once again do nothing for Anglo-Korean relations with another reference to the culinary preferences of Park Ji-Sung's fellow countrymen.]

Funnies

⚽ 'WE WANNA KNOW'

'What have I actually done? On the football side my record isn't that bad, there are others a lot worse, but the slightest thing I do just gets blown out of all proportion,' says Lee Bowyer. Time to refresh the memory: Bowyer has had more scrapes with the authorities than he's had England caps. There's the failed drugs test in 1994, the conviction for affray after an alleged racist incident in a McDonald's restaurant, the charge of GBH – later cleared – while at Leeds and his fight with team-mate Kieron Dyer at Newcastle.

Bowyer played for Birmingham in the Premier League in the 2009/10 season and it was no surprise this song sprung up, just like it did when he was with the Blues in the Championship:

Lee, Lee Bowyer!
Ooh, aah!
I wanna know why you're not in jail!

[To the tune of 'Hey Baby', by DJ Otzi. Joey Barton also often gets the DJ Otzi treatment.]

⚽ PANTS DOWN

During a court case involving Bowyer, the then Leeds midfielder admitted he was not wearing any

pants. When the defence counsel – or brief, if you will – asked Bowyer if he was wearing anything 'down there', he meekly replied 'no' while looking sheepishly at the public gallery. Unsurprisingly, Leeds United fans serenaded Bowyer with this one the next time he stepped out on to the pitch:

He's here, he's there
He wears no underwear
Lee Bowyer, Lee Bowyer!

⚽ 'AND IT'S DUBERRY'S FAULT'

More Leeds-related courtroom stories, and a tale about Michael Duberry. 'Dubes' was once loved in Yorkshire, but when he gave evidence against team-mates Jonathan Woodgate and Lee Bowyer in an assault case, he was seen as a 'grass'. Duberry eventually left Elland Road and the fickle fans have gone from loving the former Chelsea star to despising him. When Leeds went 1–0 down at Wycombe in August 2009, the travelling supporters goaded Duberry with:

1–0… and it's Duberry's fault!

[To the tune of 'Go West' by the Pet Shop Boys.]

⚽ 'TEN MEN AND THEIR MOBILE PHONES'

The *News of the World* had to apologise and pay damages to Ashley Cole in 2006 after insinuating that he took part in a gay sex orgy that involved a radio DJ and a mobile phone. But while it was clear no orgy involving Cole actually took place, try telling that to thousands of fans up and down the country:

One man went to bed
Went to bed with Ashley!
One man and his mobile phone
Went to bed with Ashley!

…continues with two men, three men, four…

Ten men went to bed
Went to bed with Ashley
Ten men and their mobile phones
Went to bed with Ashley!

[To the tune of the Chelsea anthem, 'One Man Went to Mow'.]

⚽ 'COS ASHLEY WANTS HIS BUM

When a rumour about a player's sexuality springs up, fans will never let the man in question forget about it. It's not big and it's not clever… but that's

never stopped a football fan from indulging in a bit of player-baiting. Arsenal fans again tried to wind Cole up when Lassana Diarra moved from Chelsea to north London in 2007:

Diarra, whoa!
Diarra, whoa!
He left the Chelsea scum
'Cos Ashley wants his bum!

⚽ 'UGLY TREE'

Fedde Le Grand's 'Put Your Hands Up For Detroit' forms the basis of a popular Liverpool chant for Dirk Kuyt (see 'Hero Worship'), but this next one is every bit as amusing. Strangely, the Liverpool fans sing this themselves:

Dirk Kuyt, as good as he may be
Hit every branch on the ugly tree
Like Fowler, Crouch and Craig Bellamy
Dirk Kuyt's boss but he's fucking ugly

[To the tune of 'Lord of the Dance'.]

⚽ 'YOUR WIFE'

Harry Kewell's wife Cheree Murphy got him into all sorts of trouble when she went on the reality

TV show *I'm a Celebrity... Get Me Out of Here!*

Aside from talking about his 'soft, peachy bum', she also had to eat a kangaroo testicle during one of the Bushtucker Trials. Harry had to endure the predictable terrace torment when he stepped out on to the pitch:

Your wife eats testicles!
Your wife eats testicles!

[To the tune of Giuseppe Verdi's opera 'Rigoletto'.]

⚽ 'YOU'RE WELSH'

The unique thing about Chester's Deva Stadium is that it crosses the border from England to Wales. With this in mind, it gives visiting fans ample opportunity to mock Chester supporters' heritage and question their nationality:

You're Welsh, and you know you are!

[To the tune of 'Go West' by The Pet Shop Boys.]

⚽ 'ONE SHOE'

More Pet Shop Boys tributes now and a wonderful song with a cracking story to boot. First, here's a Dundee United favourite, sung at Rangers:

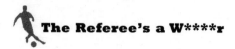

One shoe! You've only got one shoe!

[The story goes that some shoe shops in Glasgow only display the left shoe in their window displays, as the stereotypically light-fingered Glaswegians would start nicking from the shops if they put a full pair on show!]

⚽ 'WHO LET THE FROGS OUT?'

With Thierry Henry, Patrick Vieira, Nicolas Anelka and Emmanuel Petit being just a few Gallic superstars to don the Arsenal shirt, it's fair to say that Monsieur Wenger's sides have had more French flair than a night at the Moulin Rouge. So when the Baha Men stormed the music charts with their 'Who Let the Dogs Out?' hit in 2000, the chance to mock the Gunners and the French in one fell swoop proved too good an opportunity to miss.

Who let the frogs out? Who, who, who?

[To the tune of 'Who Let the Dogs Out?' by the Baha Men.]

⚽ 'YOU SHOULD HAVE STAYED ON THE TELLY'

Why did Alan Shearer give up his cushy place on the *Match of the Day* sofa to sip from the poisoned

chalice that is the Newcastle United manager's job? His decision to bid farewell to nights in with Gary Lineker backfired spectacularly and, as he trudged towards the tunnel following a typically meek surrender at Liverpool towards the end of the 2008/09 season, he was met with chants of:

You should've stayed on the telly!

['Guantanamera', before you ask!]

⚽ DUTCH SCHTEVE...

Steve McClaren, chief wrecker of the English summer in 2008, escaped to Dutch side FC Twente following his disastrous time in charge of the Three Lions. McClaren, ahead of his return to England for a Champions League qualifier against Arsenal, genuinely sounded like this in the pre-match interview:

'Championsh League, Liverpool or Arshenal, I thought one of them we would draw and it is Arshenal I think.

'To experiensh big gamesh, Championsh League... Arshenal... The Emiratesh... will be fantashtic for the playersh, not just for now but for the future ash well. I shay I think we are not just... what you call?... underdogsh but mashive underdogsh.'

The Referee's a W****r

His pseudo-Dutch accent was utterly dreadful, much like FC Twente's performance when they found themselves on the wrong end of a 4–0 crushing at the Emirates. The home fans piled on the pain for McClaren with:

You let your language down!

[To the tune of Giuseppe Verdi's opera 'Rigoletto'.]

⚽ 'WE CAN'T SEE YOU'

Following the postponement of their clash with Dagenham in March 2009 because of floodlight failure, Brentford fans kept their spirits up with this amusing take on a classic chant:

We can't see you sneaking out!
We can't see you sneaking out!

[To the tune of 'Bread of Heaven'. 'We can see you sneaking out' is usually sung to opposition fans when their team is being pummelled, as disillusioned supporters leave early to avoid further embarrassment.]

⚽ 'YOUR COAT'S FROM MATALAN'

During his time as Chelsea manager, Jose Mourinho

guided the Blues to back-to-back Premier League titles, the League Cup and the FA Cup. He will always be remembered for his entertaining press conferences and downright arrogance – and also his impressive collection of coats. But opposition supporters were less than impressed with his choice of clothing:

Your coat's from Matalan!

[To the tune of Giuseppe Verdi's opera 'Rigoletto'.]

⚽ HAVANT AND WATERLOOVILLE

The non-league club captured everyone's hearts during a memorable FA Cup run in 2008. Havant shocked Swansea to set up a trip to Liverpool in the fourth round. Fans, pundits and even the Havant players were expecting Liverpool to plunder goal after goal, but they were spectacularly wrong. Incredibly, the part-timers took the lead – twice! At 1–0 and 2–1, one of the biggest shocks in cup history looked, unbelievably, to be on. And didn't the Havant fans love it! The stadium rang with two classics:

Can we play you every week?

And…

Are you Swansea in disguise?

[Top work from the Havant supporters, although their team did eventually lose the match 5–2.]

⚽ TAKING 'CAN WE PLAY YOU EVERY WEEK?' TO THE NEXT LEVEL...

Curiously, Shamrock Rovers provided the opposition as Cristiano Ronaldo made his Real Madrid debut in 2009. With fellow big-money signing Karim Benzema also on the field, the Irish league team were expected to be on the wrong end of a cricket score. Funnily enough, things didn't turn out that way. OK, the game finished 1–0 to Madrid, but only after Benzema's scruffy late winner. During the match, Shamrock were in high spirits and chants of 'Can we play you every week?' sprung up!

⚽ 'THAT'S WHY WE LET YOU GO'

Jermain Defoe scored 19 goals in 31 highly impressive games while at Bournemouth between 2000/01 and when his loan spell expired, he moved back to West Ham and then on to Tottenham.

While Spurs went on to lift the Carling Cup and continue to enjoy forays into Europe, Bournemouth struggled to stay afloat and, in 2009, almost dropped out of the Football League.

Perhaps the Cherries could have done with Defoe? Not a chance. During a pre-season match between Spurs and the Seasiders, the striker missed a golden opportunity, giving his former club something to smile about:

That's why we let you go!
That's why we let you go!

[To the tune of Giuseppe Verdi's opera 'Rigoletto'.]

⚽ 'I WILL SURVIVE'

Gordon Strachan bounced straight back into Premier League management following relegation with Coventry in 2001 with a job at Southampton. The Saints' sworn south-coast enemies, Portsmouth, remained in the second tier of English football, but at least Pompey fans came up with this superb version of 'I Will Survive':

At first I was afraid, I was petrified
Thought I'd never get another job with a Premiership side
And I spent so many nights thinking I'd done nothing wrong
But I grew strong
And a new job came along...

The Referee's a W****r

And so I'm back! Managing the Saints!
They think I'm gonna save them but it's obvious I ain't
They should have called on Howard Wilko, Harry R or Georgie G
If they want a decent gaffer then it sure as hell ain't me!

But I will survive! I will survive!
As long as I've mates on telly I know I'll stay alive
The new Saints boss job is mine and I've crap players yet to sign
I will survive! I will survive!

[This goes against the 'keep it simple' rule of chanting, but, come on, the rhymes are brilliant!]

⚽ 'THAT'S ZAMORA'

When Bobby Zamora scored a stunning goal in Fulham's 2–0 win against Bolton in early September 2009, the Cottagers' fans thought the £4.8 million they had spent on him was starting to look like loose change. But then the goals dried up. Bobby couldn't hit a barn door and, after his spectacular strike against Bolton, went 23 Premier League games without scoring. So it came as no surprise when opposing fans caught on to his measly goal return by chanting:

When you're sat in row Z
And the ball hits your head...
That's Zamora!

[To the tune of 'That's Amore' by Dean Martin.]

Earlier in his career, Bobby couldn't stop scoring – he netted 76 goals in 129 league appearances for Brighton between 2000/03, earning him a more complimentary version of the same song:

When the ball hits the goal
It's not Yorke, it's not Cole
It's Zamora!

⚽ 'HE'S GOING GREEN IN A MINUTE'

Givanildo Vieira de Souza, better known as 'Hulk' for his striking resemblance to the fictional character, was met with this great tribute during Porto's Champions League clashes with Arsenal and Manchester United in the 2008/09 season:

He's going green in a minute!

[You've guessed it – 'Guantanamera'.]

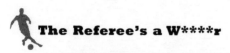

⚽ 'COULDN'T HANDLE HIS STELLA'

Staying up late and getting sozzled before a World Cup qualifier against Holland is not the wisest thing to do, as Rangers and Scotland goalkeeper Allan McGregor found to his cost. McGregor and drinking buddy Barry Ferguson were axed from the game as well as the next clash against Iceland – where the pair appeared to make V-signs at the cameras. The Rangers duo have been told they will never play for Scotland again. Still, chin up, chaps, the Tartan Army still love you – and McGregor in particular. Perhaps it's because his surname vaguely rhymes with the name of a lager:

Allan, Allan McGregor, he couldn't handle his Stella!

[To the tune of 'Abracadabra' by the Steve Miller Band.]

⚽ 'THE GAZA'S NOT YOURS'

The Gaza's not yours! The Gaza's not yours!
No Yossi Benayoun, the Gaza's not yours!

[Opposition fans get all political towards Liverpool's Israeli star Yossi Benayoun.]

⚽ 'YOU DON'T KNOW WHAT YOU'RE DOING'

Rarely does the whole stadium unite and sing in unison. While the battle unfolds on the pitch, fans are usually engaged in verbal jousting, with both sets eager to score points off each other.

But on the odd occasion when supporters gather together and sing for a common cause, the results are spectacular. Witness this gem from Leeds and Derby fans during a Carling Cup clash in 2008. When a loved-up bloke stood up and proposed to his missus during the half-time interval, both sets of fans united to sing:

You don't know what you're doing!

⚽ 'BEES UP'

With Brentford on the brink of promotion from League Two in 2009 and Luton all but relegated to the Blue Square Premier, the Bees rubbed it in through the medium of song:

Bees up Luton down! Bees up Luton down!
Bees up Luton, Bees up Luton
Bees up Luton down!

[To the tune of 'Knees up Mother Brown'.]

 **The Referee's a W****r**

⚽ 'YOUR MUM...'

Cheeky AFC Wimbledon fans deserve their inclusion in the Funnies section with this witty put-down to university side Team Bath:

Mum does your laundry!

[To the tune of Giuseppe Verdi's opera 'Rigoletto'.]

⚽ 'IF YOU LOVE GOLDEN WONDER'

Leicester's move to the Walkers Stadium may have netted them a crisp note or two, but travelling supporters are quick to point out where their snack allegiances lie:

If you love Golden Wonder clap your hands!

[To the tune of 'She'll Be Coming Round the Mountain'.]

⚽ 'WE'RE ONLY HERE...'

Never underestimate fans' ability to do some digging. Upon finding out that Rotherham's Don Valley Stadium was originally used for athletics, Leeds supporters came up with this clever put-down, sung, once again, to the tune of 'Guantanamera'.

We're only here for the shot put!

⚽ 'OH MY GOD'

Leeds score points (for once) with this fantastic double whammy of terrace humour, starting with a variation on Kaiser Chiefs' 'Oh My God', which is sung when the team are playing well away from home:

Oh my God I can't believe it
We've never been this good away from home!

In the space of six years, Leeds United fell from gracing the semi-finals of the Champions League to the third tier of English football. What Leeds players may have lacked in ability on the pitch, however, their fans more than made up for off it:

We're shit!
And we know we are!

[To the tune of 'Go West' by the Pet Shop Boys. The chant is a variation on the classic 'You're shit', sung by opposition fans to a team that's suffering on the pitch.]

Dennis Wise was the man in charge following Leeds' slip into League One in 2007 and opposition fans rubbed it in with a rousing rendition of:

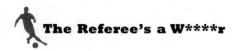

The Referee's a W****r

Wise, Wise
Whatever have you done?
You've taken Leeds to Division One
You won't win a cup, you won't win a shield!
Your biggest match will be Hudd-ers-field!

[To the tune of 'The Lord of the Dance'.]

⚽ 'DOES THE CIRCUS KNOW YOU'RE HERE?'

Peter Crouch has his fair share of admirers, but there are still those who want to laugh at his gangly frame. Luton fans were very harsh to Crouchy when he lined up for Liverpool at Kenilworth Road in an FA Cup third round tie in 2006 – but you can't help but laugh at their abuse:

Does the circus know you're here?
Does the circus! Does the circus!
Does the circus know you're here?

[To the tune of 'Bread of Heaven'.]

⚽ 'GET YOUR MASCOT OFF'

Another lower-league gem, courtesy of AFC Hornchurch fans during their FA Cup first round tie with Peterborough in 2008:

Get your mascot off the pitch!

[To the tune of 'Bread of Heaven' and directed at pint-sized Peterborough star Dean Keates.]

⚽ 'CHAS AND DAVE'

What would fans do without 'Guantanamera'? One thing's for sure, without it Spurs fans wouldn't be able to slate Manchester City fans Liam and Noel Gallagher, of Oasis:

You're just a shit Chas and Dave!

⚽ MICHAEL OWEN

Owen must have thought all his Christmases, birthdays and Bar Mitzvahs had come at once when, out of nowhere, Manchester United offered him the chance to salvage his career in the summer of 2009. Prior to their shock move for the perennially injured striker, Hull City and Stoke were interested in Owen, having been impressed with the somewhat cringeworthy sales brochure his management team had circulated in a bid to find poor Mickey a new club.

Things went badly for Owen during his final season at Newcastle – injuries, loss of form and relegation all contributed to his omission from the England setup under Fabio Capello.

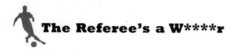

The Referee's a W****r

Eager to laugh at his poor injury record, fans constantly castigated the former Real Madrid and Liverpool star. When he did manage to limp out on to the pitch, Owen was met with a rousing rendition of:

In for a week, out for a month
In for a week, out for a month
In for a week, out for a month
Owen is a tampon!

[To the tune of 'Skip to my Lou'.]

⚽ NON-FLYING DUTCHMAN

Dennis Bergkamp was blessed with sublime skill and a knack for scoring some incredible goals during his career. Put the playmaker in front of a fearsome defence and he would find a way to slip through and score. Put him anywhere near an aeroplane, however, and he would scarper quicker than you could say 'long-haul flight':

There's only one British Airways!

[Dennis was constantly reminded about his fear of flying during his time in England. Perhaps the funniest instance of this chant came at St James's Park in 2002. The Toon Army were bellowing it

from the Gallowgate End – minutes before Bergkamp silenced them with a stunning individual goal that is surely ranked in the Premier League's all-time top five.]

⚽ 'HIS NAME IS RIO'

In 2003, Rio Ferdinand forgot to take a routine drug test and was fined £50,000 as well as receiving an eight-month ban. It meant the Manchester United defender missed Euro 2004 as well as a huge chunk of the domestic season.

Rio insisted he had simply forgotten to go and pee in a cup because he was moving house, but his appeal was rejected, leaving the England star facing up to the lengthy ban.

It came as no surprise, then, to hear this variation on Duran Duran's 'Rio':

His name is Rio and he watches from the stand!

Or, for the cynics among us:

He's out the England squad, and we know why
Cos Rio got high, Rio got high, Rio got high!

[To the tune of 'Cos I Got High' by Afroman.]

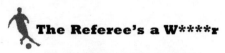

⚽ 'STAYED IN A BURGER'

As we have seen, if a footballer has a dodgy surname, he's bound to get it in the neck. Ladies and gentleman, introducing Bristol City goalkeeper Dean Gerken:

Stayed in a burger!
You should've stayed in a burger!

[To the tune of 'Guantanamera'.]

And the abuse continues, this time to the tune of 'Go West' by the Pet Shop Boys:

Your dad… is a cucumber!

⚽ 'DODGY DVD'

Zheng Zhi has since left Charlton, but the Addicks' chant for the Chinaman will live long in the memory. So, get ready to stick two fingers up at political correctness:

Zheng Zhi, wherever you may be
You sell dodgy DVDs
Could be worse
You could be a Wall
Selling crack in primary school!

[To the tune of 'Lord of the Dance'. 'Wall' refers to Charlton's south London rivals, Millwall.]

⚽ 'CARRA'S BIT ON THE SIDE'

Credit to Everton for this hilarious, if ever-so-slightly politically incorrect, remix of 'The Animals Went In Two-by-Two' aimed at Liverpool striker Fernando Torres:

He's half a girl and half a boy
Torres! Torres!
He looks just like a transvestite
Torres! Torres!
He wears a frock, he loves the cock
He sells his arse on Albert Dock
Fernando Torres, Carra's bit on the side!

['Carra' refers to Liverpool defender Jamie Carragher.]

Liverpool have their own version of this song, which they sing to Manchester City striker Carlos Tevez:

His neck scars prove he lost his head
Tevez! Tevez!
You'll never shag a sexy bird
Tevez! Tevez!
You ugly twat, you dirty c**t
They've sewn your head on back-to-front,

Carlos Tevez, Herman Munster's son!

[Herman Munster is a fictional character from the sitcom *The Munsters*. He looks a bit like Lurch from the *Addams Family*.]

⚽ 'GIVE HIM A CHANCE'

This almost got into the 'Heroes' section, but (a) David Ngog could hardly be described as a Liverpool hero and (b) it's just too funny to leave out. Sung to the tune of 'Liverpool's Number Nine' tribute to Fernando Torres (that one *is* in 'Heroes'):

His heartbeat proved he was a Red
Ngog! Ngog!
It proudly beated through the crest
Ngog! Ngog!
We bought the lad from sunny France
C'mon lads… give him a chance!
David Ngog, Liverpool's 24!

⚽ INNUENDO

When a jobsworth steward confiscated a beach ball from the crowd during a match between Oxford and Bradford in 1996, once again fans from both sides put their differences aside to sing this witty comeback:

One ball!
You've only got one ball!
You've only got one ball!

⚽ 'DUNC AND DISORDERLY'

A (very brief) history of Duncan Ferguson's personal life:

He's had four convictions for assault, including two as a result of fighting in a taxi rank and another following a brawl with a fisherman in a pub. After headbutting Raith Rovers' John McStay while playing for Rangers in 1994, Ferguson was sent to Barlinnie prison for three months as it was his fourth conviction. His house was the subject of a burglary attempt in 2001 – Big Dunc caught the perpetrators and battered them. One of the ne'er-do-wells spent three days in hospital.

Big Dunc inspired many a fan to sing a song about him, but Finnish composer Osmo Tapio Raihala went one further when he wrote an opera about the Scot's time in prison. Raihala said: 'It takes into account the contradictions in him: he has an aggressive side, but there is a lyrical undertone to him.'

The Finn wasn't the only one to convey Ferguson's colourful history creatively. During his time at Everton, the striker became a cult figure and

Toffees fans would often rise to their feet for a rendition of:

Drink, drink, wherever he may be
He is the Dunc and dis-or-der-ly
And he will drink, wherever he may be
'Cos he is the Dunc and dis-or-der-ly

[To the tune of 'Lord of the Dance'.]

⚽ LIVERPOOL

As we all know, Liverpool manager Rafael Benitez loves facts. Hands up who can remember his memorable 'fact' rant directed towards Manchester United manager Sir Alex Ferguson in the 2008/09 season? It was comic stuff.

Here's another fact for Señor Benitez, courtesy of the *Liverpool Echo* from March 2009: 'More than 52,000 are now collecting the dole in the Liverpool city region, according to official figures released today…'

The Merseysiders suffer a torrent of abuse, home and away. Eager to poke fun and jump on the 'let's reinforce the Scouse stereotype' bandwagon, rival fans have dreamt up some wonderful put-downs over the years. While Liverpool have their 'You'll Never Walk Alone' anthem, rival fans have come up with a memorable variation:

Sign on, sign on
With a pen in your hand
'Cos you'll never get a job!
You'll never get a job!
Sign on! Sign on!

'Bread of Heaven' gets a re-working as well:

Get to work you lazy twats!

As does 'You Are My Sunshine':

You are a Scouser
A thieving Scouser
You're only happy on Giro day!
Your mum's out thieving! Your dad's drug-dealing!
Please don't take my hubcaps away!

Scousers may get riled with the 'thieving' tag, but a brief glance through the crime-history books on Merseyside would go some way to telling them why such songs are commonplace on the terraces.

DECEMBER 2007 – Dirk Kuyt becomes the fifth Liverpool player in 18 months to have his home burgled.
JUNE 2006 – Jerzy Dudek had his Porsche car, jewellery and Champions League-winners' medal nicked from his home while on holiday.

JULY 2006 – Wayne Rooney's BBC Young Sports Personality of the Year award was nicked from his parents' home in Liverpool.

SEPTEMBER 2006 – Daniel Agger's Wirral home was targeted and, in the same month, Peter Crouch's house in Alderley Edge was swooped upon.

MAY 2006 – Pepe Reina was burgled while he was busy saving penalties in Liverpool's Champions League semi-final against Chelsea. Jewellery, a Bang and Olufsen entertainment system, personal documents and a grey Porsche Cayenne with Spanish number plates were taken.

⚽ 'ONE JOB'

Continuing the theme of singing about unemployment, Middlesbrough fans deserve a quick mention and a pat on the back for a witty tribute to striker Joseph Desire Job, while also poking fun at themselves:

One Job on Teesside! There's only one Job on Teesside!

[To the tune of 'Guantanamera'!]

Let's back the next song up with another fact: in 2008, the Health is Wealth Commission, set up by the University of Liverpool, ranked Liverpool as the

most deprived place in England. Despite the city being named the European capital of culture, the report put Liverpool as the most deprived region out of 354 towns and cities across England. Hence:

In your Liverpool slums! In your Liverpool slums!
You look in the dustbin for something to eat!
You find a dead rat and you think it's a treat!
In your Liverpool slums!

In your Liverpool slums! In your Liverpool slums!
Your mum's on the beat and your dad's in the nick!
You can't find a job 'cos you're so fucking thick!
In your Liverpool slums!

Or:

Feed the Scousers! Let them know it's Christmas time!

[To the tune of 'Do They Know It's Christmas' by Band Aid.]

Or:

Who can rob your houses?
(Who can rob your houses?)
Violate your gran?
(Violate your gran?)

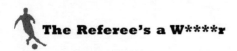 **The Referee's a W****r**

Sell cocaine from an ice-cream van?
A Scouser can!

[To the tune of 'The Candyman Can' from the *Charlie and the Chocolate Factory* film.]

⚽ 'SIT DOWN PINOCCHIO'

Carrying on the Scouser-baiting, fans up and down the country loved to goad Liverpool assistant manager Phil Thompson during his time in charge, paying particular attention to a striking facial feature:

Sit down Pinocchio!

[To the tune of Giuseppe Verdi's opera 'Rigoletto'.]

Or:

Oh the shadow outside is frightening
Stops the sun from shining in
You see it wherever he goes
Thompson's nose, Thompson's nose, Thompson's nose!

[To the tune of 'Let it Snow', by Frank Sinatra.]

⚽ 'OVER-ELABORATING'

This is pure class. Arsenal may have a reputation for playing wonderful attacking football, but, at times, they have also angered their fans for seemingly wanting to walk the ball into the back of the net as opposed to taking a punt from outside the box. Fulham supporters picked up on this during their first season in the Premier League in 2001/02 and came up with this brilliant, suitably elaborate put-down:

Same old Arsenal...
Always over-elaborating in the penalty area!

[This is sung to the standard 'same old [team], always cheating' tune, but is wonderfully over-elaborate – just like Arsenal's attacking play!]

⚽ QUE SERA, SERA (AGAIN)

The decision to hold the FA Cup semi-finals at Wembley isn't exactly popular with some fans, but at least it allowed Everton supporters to give us this hit, following their 2–1 quarter-final victory over Middlesbrough in 2009:

Tell me Ma, me Ma
To put the champagne on ice

The Referee's a W****r

We're going to Wembley twice!
Tell me Ma, me Ma!

⚽ DELUSIONAL

It can be difficult at the bottom. Games may only last 90 minutes, but when you're on the wrong end of a 4–0 scoreline, it feels like the match has gone on forever. Only a stone-hearted individual could wish a relegation scrap on someone, especially at Christmas, but West Brom fans earned a lot of respect for the way they handled a difficult 2004/05 season.

The Baggies lost 4–0 at Birmingham, a result that confirmed they would be bottom of the Premiership table on Christmas Day. When Emile Heskey netted the third goal after just 30 minutes, the away fans could have been forgiven for leaving early. A football fan is a different type of beast, however, and, realising their situation was desperate, the West Brom fans attempted to lift each other's spirits – and succeeded brilliantly:

The Premier League! (The Premier League!)
Is upside down! (Is upside down!)
The Premier League is upside down!
West Brom are top and Chelsea are bottom!
The Premier League is upside down!

Their excellent piece of gallows humour was then followed up with a rendition of:

Championé! Championé!
Olé Olé Olé!

Eager not to be outdone, Grimsby fans took their 5–0 defeat at Lincoln in 2006 with equal good humour. As Marvin Robinson smashed home the fourth goal with half-time still to come, Mariners fans saw the funny side:

Let's pretend we scored a goal!
Let's pretend! Let's pretend!
Let's pretend we scored a goal!

['Bread of Heaven', again. This was followed by the fans going crazy, shouting and cheering as if Grimsby had in fact scored.]

⚽ BRIGHTON...

...is the gay capital of Great Britain, which gives any fan unlucky enough to visit the dilapidated Withdean Stadium plenty of ammunition for a whole raft of ever-so-slightly homophobic chants:

Does your boyfriend know you're here?
Does your boyfriend know you're here?

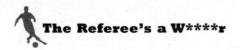

[To the tune of 'Bread of Heaven'.]

Stand up… 'cos you can't sit down!

[It's 'Go West' again…]

We can see you holding hands!

[…and it's back to 'Bread of Heaven'.]

Credit to the Seagulls fans, though. Their witty response to these chants is a 'Bread of Heaven' adaptation of their own:

You're too ugly to be gay!

⚽ 'IT'S BLUE, IT'S SQUARE'

Poor Chester City. Their financial woes and poor performances on the pitch all conspired against them in 2008/09 and left the City fans facing up to life outside the Football League. Eager to rub their noses in it, Aldershot supporters made it clear to City what fate they would face during a League Two clash between the teams in April 2009:

It's blue, it's square
You're going down to there!
Con-fer-ence! Con-fer-ence!

[To the tune of 'He's here, he's there, he's every-fucking-where'.]

Chester's fans refused to lie down, though, and came up with this brilliant retort:

We've won it before, we've won it before... in 2004, we've won it before!
We'll win it again, we'll win it again... in 2010, we'll win it again!

⚽ GUANTANAMERA...

...is clearly the football fans' theme tune of choice. This particular adaptation comes courtesy of Aston Villa supporters, who mocked Manchester United during the first half of a Premier League clash back in 2002. Olof Mellberg had just opened the scoring for Villa and, with 10 minutes of the first half to go, some home supporters had already vacated their seats:

Time for a sandwich!
It must be time for a sandwich!

[Old Trafford has former idol Roy Keane to thank for this put-down. The midfield dynamo lashed out at the home fans for the perceived lack of atmosphere at Old Trafford in 2000. Referring to those who did not sing enough (or at all) at home, he said:

'Sometimes you wonder, do they understand the game of football? Away from home our fans are fantastic, I'd call them the hardcore fans, but at home they have a few drinks and probably the prawn sandwiches, and they don't realise what's going on out on the pitch. I don't think some of the people who come to Old Trafford can spell "football", never mind understand it.']

'Bread of Heaven' would probably take the number two spot in a list of fans' favourite tunes, and another absolute classic re-working arrived in the 1990s during roly-poly Jan Molby's time at Liverpool:

Get your tits out for the lads!
Get your tits out, get your tits out
Get your tits out for the lads!

⚽ 'WITH A WALKING STICK AND A ZIMMER FRAME...'

Charlton fans were quick to slate old-timer Teddy Sheringham during a match against Colchester United in 2007. He may have won numerous titles – including a Champions League medal – but Charlton supporters clearly didn't have respect for their elders:

There's only one Teddy Sheringham! One Teddy Sheringham!

With a walking stick and a zimmer frame
Sheringham's pissed himself again!

⚽ 'THERE'S ONLY ONE JACK FROST'

Some of the most hilarious chants are those that
have a noticeable effect on play – or, in this case,
filming. During a pre-season friendly between
Chesterfield and Partick Thistle in 2000, television
cameras were filming an episode of Scotland's
favourite crime-fighting drama, *Taggart*. Eager to
pledge allegiance to their number one good guy of
choice, the Chesterfield fans constantly interrupted
filming with:

One Jack Frost!
There's only one Jack Frost!

⚽ 'SUPER CASINO? YOU'RE HAVING A LAUGH'

When the government announced plans for a Las
Vegas-style casino to be built somewhere in England,
Blackpool was the favourite destination with the
bookies. The seaside resort eventually lost out to
Manchester, prompting a typical response among
those travelling to watch their team play Blackpool:

Super Casino? You're having a laugh!

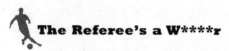

⚽ 'YOU'RE NOT AS GOOD AS CHRISTMAS'

A simple but sublime little gem from Stockport County, referring to Wycombe striker Jermaine Easter:

You're not as good as Christmas!

⚽ 'THE AUTOGLASS TROPHY'

Stoke City supporters were in good voice during their first Premier League match with Liverpool in 2008 and they had good reason to be. The five-time European Cup winners found it increasingly difficult to break down a resilient Potters defence and Tony Pulis' men came away with a credible goalless draw.

On the subject of five European Cups, here was the Stoke response to Liverpool's 'We've won it five times' song:

We've won it two times
We've won it two times!
The Autoglass Trophy!
We've won it two times!

⚽ 'WHO'S UP MARY BROWN?'

Delving into the history books, this brilliant take on 'Knees Up Mother Brown' was found, courtesy of those excellent songsmiths from Manchester.

The story goes that Tommy Docherty was sacked as Manchester United manager in 1977 because the club found out he had been having an illicit affair with physio Laurie Brown's wife Mary. Docherty was eventually shipped out. Upon hearing the news, the United fans were quick to come up with:

Doc's up Mary Brown!
Doc's up Mary Brown! Doc's up Mary, Doc's up Mary!
Doc's up Mary Brown!

⚽ 'VERA'S DEAD!'

In a tear-jerking, emotionally charged episode of *Coronation Street* in 2008, Jack Duckworth came back home from the Rovers to find his lifeless wife Vera.

So, as people around the globe came to terms with Vera's passing, it came as no surprise when those cheeky East End scamps at West Ham travelled to Manchester City and started to sing.

Vera's dead! Vera's dead! Vera's dead!

[To the tune of terrace classic 'Here We Go'.]

⚽ THIS IS NOT JUST SHOPLIFTING, IT'S MARKS AND SPENCER'S SHOPLIFTING...

John Terry's mum was arrested and cautioned in 2009 after being caught with £800 of clothes and groceries from Tesco and Marks & Spencer. Among the items in Sue's possession were said to be flip flops, leggings, casual shirts, men's and ladies' watches, a green tracksuit and groceries, including sweets and pet food.

Picking up on the pet food angle, Terry was met with all manner of 'your mum's a dog' chants when news of Sue's five-finger discount broke. West Ham fans were particularly welcoming to the England captain when he appeared at Upton Park:

Terry's mum is a dog/thief*
Is a dog, is a dog
Terry's mum is a dog
She loves Tesco!

*delete as applicable

[To the tune of 'London Bridge is Falling Down'.]

Mr Terry is no shrinking violet, especially when people sing songs about his dear old mum. On the fans' abuse, he said: 'The referee had a quiet word with me and said, "Don't wind them up." But if they

can give they can take it, and if I can take it I can give it. That's the way it's got to be.'

⚽ 'U2'

A couple of flukey goals gave Arsenal a 2–0 first-leg victory in their Champions League qualifier against Celtic in August 2009. The Gunners emerged victorious from a notoriously difficult Celtic Park stadium and didn't they just love it:

Gone to see U2
You should've gone to see U2!

[To the tune of 'Guantanamera' yet again. Irish rockers U2 played Hampden Park on the same night Arsenal beat the Bhoys at Parkhead.]

⚽ GHOST GOAL...

The term 'ghost goal' first started to spring up following referee Stuart Atwell's cataclysmic cock-up in a match between Watford and Reading in 2008. Despite the ball clearly missing the target by about three miles, Atwell incredibly gave Reading a goal, and the match ended 2–2.

Fast forward a year and, once again, the crowd were chanting 'The referee's a wanker' during Crystal Palace's clash with Bristol City at Ashton

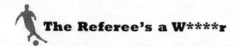

Gate. On-loan striker Freddie Sears 'scored' what looked like a legitimate goal – the ball bounced back into play having hit the back of the net. Unbelievably, referee Rob Shoebridge did not spot it, and neither did his linesman. Bristol City went on to win the match 1–0, with a goal by Nicky Maynard in the last minute. Palace were understandably furious and dubbed Bristol 'cheats' for failing to tell the ref that the Eagles had in fact scored.

The next week, when Cardiff City went 3–0 up against Bristol, the Bluebirds sang:

Win when you're cheating!
You only win when you're cheating!

Crystal Palace fans, during their 2–0 defeat to Newcastle, and still smarting from the injustice at Bristol, sang:

He's fast, he's loud
His goal was disallowed!
Freddie Sears! Freddie Sears!

And in Bristol's clash with QPR, the 'ghost goal' saga was still big news in the stands:

When the ball hits the goal
And the linesman says no...
Laugh at Warnock!

[Verdi's opera 'Rigoletto' for this one. 'Warnock', as you should know, refers to 'Mr Hard-Done-By' Neil Warnock – Crystal Palace's manager.]

Once you've wiped the tears of laughter from your eyes, get set for some Hero Worship...

CHAPTER THREE:
HERO WORSHIP

We all love a hero. Whether it's a star striker or a tireless midfield general, 3pm on a Saturday is a time to clear out the lungs and belt out odes to our favourites.

They may get paid more money than you or I (depending on how many copies this book shifts) can ever dream of, but the Premier League's star performers make us forget about our mundane nine-to-fives and our long-suffering families. Who are we to begrudge them their moment in the spotlight?

As attitudes to sex, drugs and rock and roll have become much more relaxed compared to the sepia-tinted days of yesteryear, so football chants have also taken a liberal turn. Get ready to sing about women's 'bits', offering Owen Hargreaves to your missus, an entirely predictable (yet still brilliant) festive tribute to Roque Santa Cruz, mullets and much more.

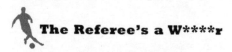

If football chants be the food of the fans, play on.

⚽ 'BALDY-HEADED WARREN FEENEY'

This is pure class – and from Luton fans no less. While the Hatters struggled to keep afloat in 2007, Warren Feeney lifted the gloom around Kenilworth Road with his distinctive appearance and whole-hearted performances. Cue:

We love our...
Itsy-bitsy, teeny-weeny
Baldy-headed Warren Feeney!

[To the tune of 'Yellow Polka-dot Bikini', which somehow became a hit for Timmy Mallett in the 1990s. The tune caught on and followed Feeney around during his days at Cardiff, Swansea and Dundee.]

⚽ 'SANTA CRUZ IS COMING TO TOWN'

Festive footie songs are like Christmas cards – they spring up around October and get consigned to the rubbish bin once everyone is sick of them. But following Roque Santa Cruz's £18 million move to Manchester City in the summer of 2009, there's every chance this hit could be here for the long haul:

You better watch out
You better beware
He's good on the ground and he's good in the air
Santa Cruz is coming to town! Santa Cruz is coming to town!
Santa Cruz is coming to town!

[To the tune of Christmas classic 'Santa Claus is Coming to Town', written by Fred Coots and Haven Gillespie and covered by everyone from Dolly Parton to Aerosmith.]

⚽ 'I'VE GOT CURLY HAIR TOO'

You've got to hand it to Owen Hargreaves. Since his big-money transfer to Manchester United in 2007 he has played just a handful of games – but the perennially sidelined midfielder has still managed to get the Stretford End masses dreaming of letting their wives soothe his injury woes.

Oh Owen Hargreaves, you are the love of my life!
Oh Owen Hargreaves, I'll let you shag my wife!
Oh Owen Hargreaves, I've got curly hair too!

[To the tune of 'Can't Take My Eyes Off You', sung by Frankie Valli.]

⚽ 'OH ANDY HUNT'

We all love a childish giggle – and Newcastle United fans provided us with one when they sung about striker Andy Hunt in the early 1990s. It caught on, and wherever Hunt went from West Brom to Charlton – he was continuously met with this great number throughout his career:

Oh Andy Hunt
He plays up front
Oh Andy Hunt, he plays up front
He's got a name like a fanny!
Oh Andy Hunt, he plays up front!

[To the tune of 'When The Saints Go Marching In', an American gospel hymn.]

⚽ 'LEAVE OUR SVEN ALONE'

Legendary lothario Sven-Göran Eriksson tugged at the heartstrings of Manchester City fans as well as Ulrika Jonsson, Faria Alam, Nancy Dell'Olio… and so on. But the Swedish sexpot (ahem) ended his love affair with City in 2008 following just one – quite successful it must be said – season in charge. And despite a creative plea to the now former owner, Thaksin Shinawatra, Sven's song fell on deaf ears.

We don't need no Phil Scolari
We don't need Mourinho
Hey! Thaksin!
Leave our Sven alone!

[To the tune of 'Another Brick in the Wall', by Pink Floyd. Sadly, 'Sinatra', as he became known at Eastlands, didn't want 'Five Minutes More' of Sven and decided 'Now is the Hour' for Mark Hughes. How 'Insensitive' of him. OK, no more now.]

⚽ 'LET'S TALK ABOUT CESC'

Sadly, this next song is as pointless as a Real Madrid defence now that most of the players featured have moved on to pastures new, but the tune still gets some airtime at the Emirates – perhaps the Gooners are trying to tell Monsieur Wenger to start getting the chequebook out?

Let's talk about Cesc, baby
Let's talk about Fla-mi-ni
Let's talk about Theo Walcott, Freddie Ljungberg and Henry!
Let's talk about Cesc!

[To the Tune of Salt 'n' Pepa's annoyingly catchy 'Let's Talk About Sex'.]

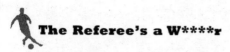

⚽ 'COME ON AND DO THE CONGA!'

Into the list comes a conga classic that is as good to watch as it is to hear. Most of the time we witness pot-bellied fanatics lauding their idols from the stands as they struggle to stand up for more than five minutes, but Aston Villa fans take singing and dancing to the next level with this simple tune:

Do-do-dooooo!
Nigel Reo-Coker!

[Repeat until bored/tired of doing the conga/told to stop doing the conga by sour-faced stewards.]

⚽ RONALDINHO

Even the world's most famous and talented players cannot avoid stick from the fans. Here's a ditty aimed at Brazil star Ronaldinho:

Cilla wants her teeth back
Cilla wants her teeth back
Tra-la-la-la! Tra-la-la-la!

[Ronaldinho may be supremely skilful but he's also sinfully ugly. Liverpool fans urged the buck-toothed one to give his gnashers back to Cilla Black during a Champions League clash against Barcelona in 2007.]

⚽ 'WE'RE HALFWAY THERE'

A few seasons ago *Soccer Saturday* presenter Jeff Stelling declared his love for Middlesbrough after it was voted the worst place to live in the UK. If you haven't already heard it, shame on you – go and visit YouTube. Sorry Jeff, but this simply brilliant song about Jérémie Aliadière is probably the best thing to come out of Teesside. And yes, that includes Captain Cook's monument, the River Tees, the Transporter Bridge, Vera Duckworth and Paul Daniels…

Oh! We're halfway there!
Whoa!
Ali-a-di-ère!

[To the tune of Jon Bon Jovi's 'Living on a Prayer'.]

⚽ 'LITTLE LORD HEALY'

Leeds United have suffered a demise of Biblical proportions. Once a Premier League force capable of reaching the Champions League semi-finals, their fall from grace is gut-wrenching for the Yorkshire club. Gone are the days of Rio Ferdinand, Harry Kewell, Mark Viduka and even David Healy, but since his exit from Elland Road, Irish strike star Healy still gets his moment in the sunshine thanks to this hymn:

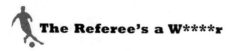The Referee's a W****r

Away in a manger
No crib for a bed
The little Lord Jesus laid down his sweet head
The stars in the bright sky
Looked down where HE LAY! HEALY! HEALY!

[To the tune of 'Away in a Manger'.]

⚽ 'RAFA'S BEARD'

The simple three-line rhyming song has become as common around the grounds as a referee's mistake and it all started with the 'He's here, he's there, he's every-fucking-where...' tribute. Liverpool fans deserve their dues here with their affection for Rafael Benitez's facial hair:

It's neat
It's weird
It's Rafa's goatee beard!
Goatee beard! Goatee beard!

Mr Benitez offered his excuses for this facial abomination in August 2007: 'The reason for my beard is that over the summer I lost my razor.'

They keep coming...

He's big, he's Red

His feet stick out the bed!
Peter Crouch! Peter Crouch!

He's big, he's mad
He dances like your dad
Peter Crouch! Peter Crouch!

[We can all remember Crouchie's 'robot' dance!]

⚽ A WORD FROM CROUCHY...

Actually, there are two very, very funny words from Crouch, but we'll leave those until the 'Extra Time' chapter. In the meantime, Crouch tells us about his favourite terrace tribute – and it's none of the above.

Instead, his favourite song came during his days as an apprentice at QPR, where he earned the nickname Rodney – after Del Boy's lanky brother in *Only Fools and Horses*.

Crouch said: 'The first song I ever heard with my name in it was sung to the *Only Fools and Horses* theme tune. It went: "No Income tax, no VAT, a 60-grand transfer fee. Black or white, rich or poor, Peter Crouch is gonna score." I thought it was a really good song!'

⚽ 'HE'S BIG, HE'S SCOUSE'

He's big, he's Scouse!

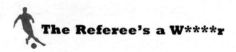

The Referee's a W****r

He's gonna rob your house!
Wayne Rooney! Wayne Rooney!

He's fast, he's Red!
He speaks like Father Ted!
Robbie Keane! Robbie Keane!

He'll shoot, he'll score!
He'll eat your labrador!
Seol Ki-Hyeon! Seol Ki-Hyeon!

[Another Korean who enjoyed cult status during his time in England. Following on from Manchester United's love for Park Ji-Sung, Reading reminded everyone that they loved Seol with this excellent rendition.]

He's bald, he's shit!
He plays when no-one's fit!
Cygan! Cygan!

[French defender Pascal Cygan never really inspired confidence during his time at Arsenal...]

⚽ THEY KEEP ON COMING...

He's big, he's fast!
His first name should be last!
Stern John! Stern John!

[Stern John is a journeyman striker, having played for Nottingham Forest, Birmingham City, Coventry, Derby County, Sunderland, Southampton and Bristol City among others. But what the Trinidadian lacked in loyalty, he more than made up for with his backwards name.]

He's fat, he's round!
He swears like Chubby Brown!
Joe Kinnear! Joe Kinnear!

[Fans up and down the country hail then Newcastle boss Joe Kinnear following his astonishing 52-swear-word rant at journalists.]

⚽ WHOA!

The classic tune 'Volare' is another fans' favourite, thanks to its terrace-friendly 'Whoa' bits. Keen not to be outdone by Liverpool (see above), Manchester United supporters are the top songsmiths here:

Nemanja! Whoa! Nemanja! Whoa!
He comes from Serbia
He'll fucking murder ya!

[Old Trafford appreciates the tough-tackling Serbian star, a man you wouldn't want to meet in a dark alley...]

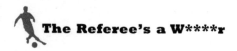

The Referee's a W****r

Kasper, whoa!
Oh Kasper, whoa!
He stands between our posts
He's named after a ghost!

[Top work, Cardiff fans. The Bluebirds came up with this when Peter Schmeichel's son, Kasper, spent a season on loan with the Welsh club in 2007/08.]

Diego! Whoa!
Diego! Whoa!
He comes from Uruguay
He made the Scousers cry!

[Diego Forlan didn't do too much during his time at Old Trafford, but he will forever be remembered on the terraces as the man who scored twice in United's 2-1 win away at Liverpool in 2002, denting the Merseysiders' title hopes in the process.]

⚽ AND MORE...

Vic Moses! Whoa!
Vic Moses! Whoa!
He comes from Norbury
He parted the Red Sea!

[Excellent work from Crystal Palace fans here, saluting local boy Victor Moses.]

Vieira! Whoa!
Vieira! Whoa!
He gave Giggsy the ball
And Arsenal won fuck all!

[Sung to Patrick Vieira after he gave the ball away against Manchester United in the last-ever FA Cup semi-final replay in 1999, before matches were decided by extra-time and penalty shoot-outs. Ryan Giggs picked up the loose pass from Vieira and scored a stunner. Arsenal lost the match 2–1 and, famously, United went on to win the Treble.]

Tom Davis! Whoa!
Tom Davis! Whoa!
He's better than Zidane
He's got a perma-tan!

[Nice. AFC Wimbledon fans show their appreciation for bronzed midfielder Tom Davis.]

Speroni! Whoa!
Speroni! Whoa!
He's got a pony-tail
His name is like an ale!

[Crystal Palace hail goalkeeper Julian Speroni, whose surname sounds mightily similar to Italian lager Peroni.]

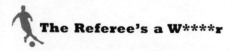
The Referee's a W****r

Sean Thornton! Whoa!
Sean Thornton! Whoa!
He likes to go out on the lash
He's better than Fab-re-gas!

[Leyton Orient midfielder Sean Thornton endured an injury hit season in the 2008/09 campaign. While he will point to hamstring strains and ankle injuries, Os fans joked he liked a beer or three.]

⚽ FABREGAS CATCHES ON...

Hot on the heels of one Fabregas song, Manchester United fans get another mention thanks to this brilliant take on the Black Lace hit 'Agadoo':

Ander-son-son-son
He's better than Kle-ber-son
Ander-son-son-son
He's our midfield ma-gi-cian!
To the left, to the right
To the Samba beat tonight
He is class, with the brass
And he shits on Fab-re-gas!

⚽ JOLLY GOOD FELLOWS...

Two wonderful variations on 'For He's a Jolly Good Fellow' – which is, by the *Guinness Book of Records'* understanding, the second most popular song in the English language, behind 'Happy Birthday'. They obviously didn't hear this version, belted out by Drogheda United supporters during Keith Fahey's time at the club:

Fahey's a jolly good fellow!

Or this, from Arsenal fans saluting Mexican Carlos Vela:

For he's a jolly good Vela!

Good work all round.

⚽ 'BOOM BOOM BOOM'

The Outhere Brothers stormed the charts with their 'Boom Boom Boom' song in the early 1990s and it left a lasting legacy.

Boom Boom Boom!
Let me hear ya say Yeo... Yeo!

[Chester fans to Simon Yeo in 2008.]

⚽ '...WILL ALWAYS LOVE YOU'

Excellent work here from Crystal Palace fans,

serenading Alessandro N'Diaye during a clash against Newcastle in August 2009, to the tune of Whitney Houston's 'I Will Always Love You':

N'Diaye… will always love you!

⚽ 'FELLAI-NI-NI-NI'

Standing at six-foot-plus and with a huge afro, it was only a matter of time before Marouane Fellaini's name was sung on the terraces at Goodison Park. Continuing the 'Agadoo' theme:

Fellai-ni-ni-ni, he is over six-foot-three
Fellai-ni-ni-ni, he's our new Lee Car-s-ley!
In the air, on the floor
Feed the Yak and he will score
He is big, he is blue
And he's coming after you!

⚽ 'OH HABIB BEYE'

Newcastle were more like *Looney Tunes* than the Toon during the 2008/09 season. Manager walk-outs, boardroom scuffles, dreadful football and the inevitable relegation that followed made it a season to forget on Tyneside. The club became a laughing stock, but at least they had one reason to smile – defender Habib Beye was one bright point in an

114

otherwise dire year and fans showed their appreciation with this gem:

Sunday, Monday, Habib Beye!
Tuesday, Wednesday, Habib Beye!
Thursday, Friday, Habib Beye!
Saturday! Habib Beye! Rocking all week with you!

[Yep, it's the *Happy Days* theme tune.]

While we're on the subject of Beye, there is a quite wonderful website, beyewatch.com, which keeps you up to date on the latest goings-on regarding the defender. Beye moved to Aston Villa in August 2009 and is a big fan of beyewatch.com: 'It's a great website, especially for the *Happy Days* song,' he says.

⚽ 'ARE YOU OKAY NANI?'

Manchester United winger Nani bares a striking resemblance to the late, great Michael Jackson, before he turned 'Bad' (sorry). Hence this corker, heard during United's Community Shield clash against Chelsea in August 2009:

Nani are you okay?
Are you okay, are you okay Nani?

[To the tune of 'Smooth Criminal' by Michael Jackson.]

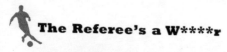

⚽ 'WHAT'S THAT COMING OVER THE HILL?'

When Tottenham fans aren't dreaming of ways to mutilate Sol Campbell, they're actually quite a nice bunch. The masses at White Hart Lane greeted Pascal Chimbonda upon his return to Spurs in 2009 with this catchy hit:

What's that coming over the hill?
Is it Chimbonda? Is it Chimbonda?

[To the tune of the Automatic's 'Monster' song. Manchester United fans also use this one to serenade scary defender Nemanja Vidić – 'What's that coming over the hill? Is it Nemanja?']

⚽ 'HE LOVES THIS CITY'

You can't escape the prowess of Liverpool and Manchester United fans when it comes to appreciating their heroes. Following on from Spurs' use of a dancefloor smash hit to laud Chimbonda comes another use of a chart-topper, this time directed at Dirk Kuyt:

Put your hands up for Dirk Kuyt
He loves this city!
Der-der-der-der-der-der! Der-der-der-der-der-der-der!

[If you haven't heard Fedde Le Grand's sensational 'Put Your Hands Up For Detroit', then the final line will make no sense to you at all.]

⚽ 'DON'T CHA WANT SOME KOMPANY?'

Apart from Nicole Scherzinger, the Pussycat Dolls don't really set the mind racing among football fans – with the exception of Manchester City. Eulogising about the talents of Belgian midfielder Vincent Kompany, the Eastlands fanatics dreamt up this catchy number inspired by one of the Dolls' chart toppers:

Don't Cha wish your midfield had Kom-pa-ny?

[To the tune of 'Don't Cha' by the Pussycat Dolls.]

⚽ 'DON'T CHA' PART TWO...

Fair play to James Beattie. Stoke fans may have questioned his arrival in January 2008, but his seven goals helped keep them in the Premier League and helped him earn a song in the process.

Don't Cha wish your striker was James Bea-tt-ie?

⚽ 'VINCE GRELLA, ELLA, ELLA'

From the Pussycat Dolls to Rihanna, Blackburn Rovers spent most of the 2008/09 season flirting with relegation and doing their best 'Umbrella' cover to sing about defender Vince Grella:

There's only one Grella, ella, ella, hey, hey!

[To the tune of Rihanna's number-one smash hit 'Umbrella'.]

Now he's playing more than ever
You can stand under my Darren Fletcher
Fletcher, Fletcher – hey, hey
Under my Darren Fletcher
Fletcher, Fletcher – hey hey!

[Good one here from Scotland supporters, reacting to Darren Fletcher's emergence in the side. The Tartan Army earn extra points for twisting more of Rihanna's 'Umbrella' lyrics.]

⚽ 'HE DRINKS SANGRIA'

Nice ode to Luis Garcia – the song really gathered momentum following his match-winning goal in the Champions League semi-final against Chelsea in 2005.

Luis Garcia
He drinks Sangria
He came from Barca to bring us joy
He's 5ft 7 from football heaven
So please don't take our Luis away!

[To the tune of 'You Are My Sunshine'.
Unfortunately for Liverpool fans, their Luis Garcia
was taken away – to Atletico Madrid in 2007.]

⚽ 'YOU DO THE MARADONA'

The Scots earn their dues for a variety of a hilarious
terrace chants in the 'Funnies' section, and here is a
quite brilliant 'Hokey Cokey' taunt from Ross County
fans, directed at Inverness manager Terry Butcher:

You put your left arm in, your left arm out,
In out, in out, shake it all about!
You do the Maradona and you turn around
That's what it's all about!
Oh Diego Maradona! Oh Diego Maradona!
Oh Diego Maradona
He put Butcher out, out, out!

⚽ IT WAS ABOUT TIME...

...Spurs fans' hatred for Sol Campbell got a mention.
Lovingly entwined amid a song about livewire

winger Aaron Lennon, the former (whisper it quietly) Arsenal defender still incurs the wrath of the White Hart Lane crowds. And they still won't stop going on about his sexuality.

You are my Lennon, my Aaron Lennon
You make me happy, when skies are grey
You're better value than Theo Walcott
And by the way Sol Campbell is gay!

[To the tune of 'You Are My Sunshine']

⚽ 'MY OLE SOLSKJAER'

In similar style to the Tottenham tune for Lennon, here's Manchester United (them again) with another 'Let's sing about our idol and slate someone else while we're at it' idea:

You are my Solskjaer, my Ole Solskjaer
You make me happy, when skies are grey
Alan Shearer was fucking dearer
Please don't take my Solskjaer away!

[Shearer, the Premier League's record goalscorer, snubbed a move to United in 1996 and the champions later bought Solskjaer for a mere £1.2 million. The Norwegian scored the winning goal in the 1999 Champions League final, while

Shearer's medal haul consists of one title success with Blackburn.]

⚽ PORN

Don't get your hopes up, chaps. Nothing smutty to see here, but get over the disappointment by belting out this excellent tribute to Emmanuel Petit, the former Arsenal and Chelsea midfielder:

He's blonde, he's quick
His name's a porno flick!
Emmanuel! Emmanuel!

[Purely for research purposes, this author wanted to find out more about this song. The blue movie connoisseurs among us will know that the flick in question is *Emmanuelle*, the lead character in a string of soft-core porn movies. Not entirely sure which *Emmanuelle* film the fans were referring to, however. There's bloody hundreds of them!]

⚽ 'WE'VE GOT TINY COX'

From porn to tiny Cox… you've got to love a bit of double entendre. Brighton fans clearly do, as they greet diminutive midfielder Dean Cox with this charming tune:

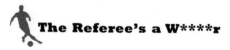

The Referee's a W****r

We've got tiny Cox!
We've got tiny Cox!
We've got tiny! We've got tiny!
We've got tiny Cox!

[Go back to 'Oldies But Goodies' and sing the 'Who ate all the pies?' song to hear how this sounds.]

⚽ 'FORMER DUTCH MARINE'

More magic from Brighton and their appreciation for goalkeeper Michel Kuipers. The Dutchman used to work in the marines before he turned to football.

In the town where I was born
Lived a man who sailed the sea
He was big, and he was Dutch
And he doesn't let in much
Michel Kuipers is a former Dutch marine!
A former Dutch marine!
A former Dutch marine!

[To the tune of 'Yellow Submarine' by the Beatles.]

⚽ 'HE PAINTS AND DECORATES'

From double entendres to Italian opera, this West Ham tribute to Paulo Di Canio sparked a glut of imitations from fans across the country, from non-

league to the Premier League. Its appeal is in its simplicity – sung to the tune of 'La donna è mobile' (Woman is fickle) from Giuseppe Verdi's opera 'Rigoletto'.

Paulo Di Can-i-o! Paulo Di Can-i-o!
PAULO DI CAN-I-O! PAULO DI CAN-I-O!

We've got Mour-in-ho, you've got my ster-e-o!
We've got Mour-in-ho, you've got my ster-e-o!

[This Mourinho tribute was first sung by Chelsea fans playing on the traditional 'thieving Scouse' stereotype away at Liverpool in 2004.]

We've got Dave Til-bu-ry
He'll paint your house for free
He quotes and estimates
He paints and decorates

[Windsor and Eton pay homage to defender Dave Tilbury, whose no-nonsense displays at the back won him the hearts of many during his time at the club.]

We don't pay council tax!
We don't pay council tax!
We don't pay council tax!
We don't pay council tax!

[University side Team Bath love singing this one to the opposing fans of professional visiting teams. Brilliant!]

Who needs Mourinho?
We've got Dave Pacio!

[Dave Pacio gets a big vote of confidence from Droylsden fans in 2008 – as his side finally won their first game of the season, at the FOURTEENTH time of asking!]

Who needs Mourinho?
We've got Tom Warrilow!

[Jose Mourinho comes in for some stick again as Tonbridge Angels fans show their appreciation to Tom Warrilow in their game against Horsham.]

⚽ 'SHOULDN'T LIGHT HIS FARTS'

Not to be outdone by opera or double entendres, West Brom fans pun their way into the book with this classic:

Bernt Haas
Shouldn't light his farts!
Bernt Haas
Shouldn't light his farts!

[To the tune of 'Go West' by the Pet Shop Boys.]

⚽ MORE 'GO WEST'

Nayim, from the halfway line!

[This particular number has been popular among Tottenham fans ever since Nayim's stunning last-minute winner for Real Zaragoza in the Cup-Winners' Cup final against Arsenal in 1995.]

Ooh aah, Eric Cantona!

[Manchester United salute the mercurial Frenchman.]

Gerard, Gerard Houllier!

[So do Liverpool.]

⚽ HOW TO UPSET MUSLIMS...

Bundesliga side Schalke cheer for their team with a rousing rendition of a song called 'Blue and White, How I Love You'.

The third verse contains the lines:

Muhammad was a prophet who understood nothing about football

But of all the lovely colours he chose [Schalke's] blue and white!

[Schalke, in western Germany's Ruhr Valley, has a large Muslim population and the song has infuriated them because of the reference to the prophet Muhammad. Whoever said Germans don't have a sense of humour?]

⚽ 'YOUR MAMA TOO'

Arsenal's adaptation of 'Let's Talk About Sex' will take some beating, but this witty one-liner sure comes close:

Ooh, stick you – your mama too – Samir Nasri!

[To the tune of 'Ooh Stick You,' by Daphne and Celeste.]

⚽ 'QUE SERA, SERA' PART THREE...

John Carew was caught in a lap-dancing club just hours before Aston Villa's UEFA Cup clash with Ajax in 2008 but far from being outraged at his lack of professionalism, the supporters viewed him as anything but a Villain.

John Carew, Carew,
He's big and he scores a few

He likes a lap-dance or two
John Carew, Carew!

[Superb stuff from the Villa fans.]

John Carew, Carew
He's bigger than me or you
He'll score us a goal, or two
John Carew, Carew

[Big John loves that particular song from the Villa followers, saying: 'It's a funny one. Maybe in a happy moment I'll find myself singing my own song in the shower.']

Carew, Carew
Carew is on fire!

[To the tune of 'The Roof is on Fire' by Rock Master Scott.]

⚽ BEST OF THE REST...

Steve Gerrard, Gerrard
He's big and he's fucking hard
He hits the ball 40 yards
Steve Gerrard, Gerrard!

[Liverpool salute skipper Stevie G.]

The Referee's a W****r

Que sera, sera,
Whatever will be, will be
We're going to Forest Green
Que sera, sera.

[Newly-relegated Wrexham fans against Hereford in 2008.]

Jim Bullard, Bullard
He's thinner than Frank Lampard
He shoots better than Steve Gerrard
Jim Bullard, Bullard

[Fulham took Jimmy Bullard to their hearts during his time at Craven Cottage. He moved to Hull City in January 2009, but the Tigers fans had to wait a while before they could adopt the song – he suffered a knee injury that ruled him out for months after only one game for his new club. Even so, it's a blinding song – so says Jimmy himself: 'I love the song, although I'm not sure I'm better than Steven. I'm definitely thinner than Frank, though.']

⚽ SORRY SOL...

...but more negative press for you again. On the upside, at least this Bolton chant about Danny Shittu isn't *too* offensive.

Chim chiminey
Chim chiminey
Chim chim cheroo!
Who needs Sol Campbell when we've got Shittu?

[To the tune of 'Chim Chiminey' from the *Mary Poppins* film.]

Tim Timminy, Tim Timminy
Tim Tim Ter-oo
We've got Tim Howard and he says 'fuck you'!

[Political correctness went right out the window when Tim Howard arrived in England. Manchester United supporters, upon hearing that the American had Tourette's syndrome, came up with this classic. Everton have since inherited it following Howard's move to Goodison Park.]

⚽ 'WHAT CAN YOU PLAY?'

Steven Pienaar has earned quite a following since his switch from Borussia Dortmund to Everton, and the Toffees fans like to serenade him with this take on a Black Lace hit:

I am the Music Man
I come from far away
And I can play (what can you play?)

The Referee's a W****r

I play the Pienaar!
Pi-a! Pi-a! Pie-naar! Pie-naar! Pie-naar! Pi-a! Pi-a!
Pie-naar! Pi-a Pie-naar!

[To the tune of 'The Music Man' by Black Lace.]

⚽ IT WAS A MATTER OF TIME...

...before another song for Sol? No, not yet – but one for
Rory Delap, whose throw-ins terrorised defences in the
Potters' debut season in the Premier League in 2008/09
and contributed to Stoke City's surprising survival.

Follow, Follow, Follow
Stoke City is the team to follow!
We've got Rory Delap
You all said he was crap!
But you just can't handle his throw!

[Lots of fans have adapted the hymn 'Follow,
Follow, We Will Follow Jesus' and sung it on their
travels or at home.]

While Stoke's football wasn't pretty, they achieved
what they set out to do in their debut season in the
Premier League and stayed up. Delap's fearsome
throw-ins led to a string of goals for the Potters,
although not everyone was pleased with Stoke's
style of play:

Come to see a throw-in
You've only come to see a throw-in!

['Guantanamera' rears its head again.]

⚽ HYMNS

From the 'Kum-ba-yah' hymn comes two versions
from the two Uniteds. Simples.

Kets-bai-ya, my Lord, Kets-bai-ya
He kicks ad-vert-boards, Kets-bai-ya
Kets-bai-ya, my Lord, Kets-bai-ya
He kicks ad-boards, Kets-bai-ya

[If you haven't seen why Newcastle fans sung this
about Temuri Ketsbaia, please do. He scored a last
minute tap-in to beat Bolton in 1998 and, well,
that's when the party *really* started.]

He scores goals galore, he scores goals
He scores goals galore, he scores goals
He scores goals galore, he scores goals
Paul Scholes, he scores goals

[Manchester United salute midfield maestro
Paul Scholes.]

⚽ 'KNOWING ME, KNOWING YOU'

Marian Pahars scored 43 league goals during his time at Southampton and the little Latvian even stayed with the club when they were relegated to the Championship in 2005. He was a loyal, livewire striker – hence the appreciation from the Saints:

Knowing me, knowing you – Pahars!
Goals are something he can do!

[To the tune of 'Knowing Me, Knowing You' by ABBA.]

⚽ 'YOU'RE SO VAIN'

Everton fans earn top marks for this one:

Leighton Baines
I bet you think this song is about you!

[To the tune of Carly Simon's 'You're So Vain'. Works perfectly with Baines, although perhaps the meaning of the song is better suited to a certain preening poser now playing in Spain…]

⚽ 'MAKES RONALDO LOOK SHITE'

On the subject of Ronaldo, the Real Madrid star failed to shine in the early part of what turned out

132

to be his final season at Manchester United. Aston Villa's Ashley Young, however, started brilliantly – leading manager Martin O'Neill to claim he was in the same class as Ronaldo and Lionel Messi. He'd obviously been listening to the Villa fans, who sang this when Young scored a brilliant last-minute winner against Everton at Goodison Park in December 2008:

He plays on the left, he plays on the ri-i-ight
Our boy Ashley
Makes Ronaldo look shite!

[To the tune of 'Sloop John B' by The Beach Boys. Following that goal against Everton, Young's manager Martin O'Neill said: 'Once Ashley puts some weight on he will be fantastic. At the moment he's about three-and-a-half stone – a couple of times we have put him through the letterbox!' Young now knows what he needs to keep on delivering... sorry.]

⚽ WHEN THEY LOVED HIM...

United fans sang numerous songs about Cristiano Ronaldo during his six years at Old Trafford. There were two versions of the 'He plays on the left...' song:

He plays on the left, he plays on the ri-i-ight
That boy Ronaldo, makes Beckham look shite!

[This one made Ronaldo's task of inheriting David Beckham's number 7 shirt a little less daunting for him. For the second version, substitute 'Beckham' for 'England'. Staunch United fans have hated England ever since the Three Lions faithful sang 'Stand up if you hate Man U' at the old Wembley. Old Trafford responded with the 'Ronaldo makes England look shite' song following the Portugeezer's brilliant displays (and winning penalty in the quarter-final) against them in the 2006 World Cup.]

⚽ WHEN THEY LOVED HIM PART TWO...

Ronaldo once heard chants of 'Viva Ronaldo... running down the wing, hear United sing', but as supporters became disenchanted with his flirtations with Madrid, they switched the lyrics to pay tribute to the Brazilian full-back twins, Rafael and Fabio Da Silva.

Viva Da Silva! Viva Da Silva!
When they're on the pitch, we don't know which is which!
Viva Da Silva!

⚽ WHEN THEY LOVED HIM PART THREE...

Before the goals dried up and he made his big-money move to Manchester City, Arsenal fans warmed to Emmanuel Adebayor. Continuing the 'Sloop John B' theme, they outdid United with one brilliant version in particular:

The baby's not yours! The baby's not yours!
No Stevie Gerrard – it's Adebayor's!

[Stevie G's WAG Alex Curran denied reports she was having the England star's second child in May 2008. The Arsenal fans obviously agreed.]

Adebayor, Adebayor!
Give him the ball – and he will score!

[Nice one this, but it has died down since Adebayor's move away from Arsenal. Flick your way to 'X-Rated' and see what they sing about him now...]

⚽ WHEN THEY LOVED HIM PART FOUR...

Dimitar Berbatov's 27 Premier League goals in two seasons – from 2006 to 2008 – really endeared the ex-Bayer Leverkusen striker to the Tottenham fans, but when the Bulgarian sulked in a bid to engineer a move to Manchester United in the 2008/09 season, the Spurs fans turned on him. Here's a reminder to Dimitar of a time when White Hart Lane loved him:

The Referee's a W****r

Ber-ba-tov, he's from Bulgaria
Ber-ba-tov, signed from Bavaria
Ber-ba-tov, great in the area
Ber-ba-tov, there's no one deadlier!

[To the tune of 'Go West' by the Pet Shop Boys. Incidentally, Tottenham should really brush up on their geography – Leverkusen is nowhere near Bavaria; it's on the eastern bank of the Rhine halfway between Cologne and Düsseldorf. Berbatov had obviously never heard of the Pet Shop Boys. During his time in Germany, he said: 'Why don't they sing my name? It's probably because my name is too difficult for them to fit into a song.']

⚽ 'TOOK ONE LOOK AT CITY'

Manchester City tried to hijack Manchester United's bid for Dimitar Berbatov on transfer-deadline day in 2008. He chose the red half of Manchester and, despite a tepid first season at Old Trafford, the fact he snubbed City saved him from further chants of 'What a waste of money'.

Di-mi-tar Ber-ba-tov
Took one look at City and he said 'fuck off'!

[To the tune of 'Jesus Christ Superstar', written by Sirs Tim Rice and Andrew Lloyd Webber.]

⚽ 'ROUND AND ROUND'

Berbatov may have snubbed City, but Real Madrid star Robinho didn't – although whether he actually realised he was going to Eastlands remains uncertain. In his press conference he said he was glad to be joining Chelsea, and had to be hastily corrected! Instead of cruising round Manchester in a new Ferrari, however, Robinho was spotted taking a trip to the Trafford Centre on the local bus – and the City fans were quick to react:

Robinho on the bus goes round and round
Round and round, round and round
Robinho on the bus goes round and round
All day long!

[To the tune of 'The Wheels on the Bus', a children's classic.]

The wheels on your house go round and round
Round and round, round and round
The wheels on your house go round and round
All day long!

[Heard at Gillingham's Priestfield Stadium throughout 2007. The Gills fans have a banner that reads 'Pikey Army', a slang term that refers to travellers.]

 **The Referee's a W****r**

⚽ THEY'LL ALWAYS LOVE HIM

Andy Cole is the Premier League's second all-time leading goalscorer, just behind Alan Shearer. He banged them in for Newcastle and Manchester United (and to a lesser extent, Blackburn and Fulham), earning him this song:

Andy Cole, Andy Cole, Andy Andy Cole
He gets the ball, he scores a goal
Andy Andy Cole!

⚽ TIME FOR ABBA

A list of top chants is not complete without a mention from ABBA. Barnet serenaded striker Junior Agogo to the tune of 'Fernando' every time he found the net – which was relatively often.

I can feel it in the air tonight
The stars are bright
Agogo!

[Middlesbrough fans replaced Agogo with Afonso following the Brazilian's switch to the Riverside in 2008. Reckon they still sing their version? Three guesses.]

⚽ 'EL-HADJI DIOUF WILL SPIT ON YOU'

Sometimes, a player's misdemeanours can actually endear him to his fans (see John Carew's lap-dance classic). Senegal striker El-Hadji Diouf has a reputation for a dreadful dress sense, his DIOUFY numberplate and the fact that he'll spit at anything that moves.

Tra la la la la la la la! (clap, clap)
Tra la la la la la la la! (clap, clap)
Tra la la la la la la la!
El-Hadji Diouf will spit on you!

[To the tune of 'Show Me The Way to Amarillo' by Tony Christie and revived by Peter Kay, as well as Liverpool, Bolton and Blackburn fans.]

⚽ 'I PREDICT A FRYATT'

Does what is says on the tin. Matty Fryatt's free-scoring exploits propelled Leicester up the League One table in the 2008/09 season and the striker was rewarded with a simple yet effective chant:

I predict a Fryatt!

[To the tune of 'I Predict a Riot' by the Kaiser Chiefs.]

⚽ 'LOVE WILL TEAR US APART'

Hats off to Villa fans, once again. They're doing well in this book, aren't they? Their next entry is a wonderful example of gallows humour. CSKA Moscow striker Wagner Love had just netted against Martin O'Neill's men, effectively ending their UEFA Cup hopes:

Love, Love'll tear us apart, again!

[To the tune of 'Love Will Tear Us Apart' by Joy Division. Manchester United fans sing 'Giggs will tear you apart again' to show their appreciation for the Welsh wing wizard.]

⚽ 'KNIGHT FEVER'

Leon Knight had a bright career ahead of him when he signed professional terms at Chelsea – then it all went sour. Following injuries, loss of form and alleged bust-ups, he gradually made his way down the divisions and is now plying his trade with Hamilton Academical in the Scottish Premier League after a short spell in Greece. Despite his fall from grace, the Rushden and Diamonds fans still had faith in him during his time at Nene Park in 2008:

Knight fever, Knight fever

Hero Worship

He knows where the goal is!

[To the tune of 'Night Fever' by the Bee Gees.]

⚽ 'ON HIS HEAD'

Former Nottingham Forest striker Jason Lee will never be remembered for scoring goals – probably because he didn't score enough of them. What we will all remember him for is THAT haircut.

He's got a pineapple... on his head!

[To the tune of 'He's Got The Whole World In His Hands'. On his haircut and the abuse he got, Lee said: 'I'd be a liar if I said it didn't affect me. It coincided with a lack of form, which any player can have, and it grew to the extent where it was affecting people around me.' Is that the haircut or the abuse, Jason?]

⚽ ALWAYS ON MY MIND...

Time for another Jason now – former Southampton striker Jason Euell, who was last seen plying his trade at Blackpool. Euell was the best of a bad bunch at Southampton, which explains why they dropped out of the Championship in 2009. Even so, the Saints can console themselves with the fact that their song

for Jason was quite impressive – well, something had to be impressive down on the south coast.

Maybe he doesn't score them
Quite as often as he used to
Maybe he doesn't shine now
Quite as often as his shoes do
Little things that he still does with style
Like the tackle from behind
Euell is always on our mind!
Euell is always on our mind!

[To the tune of 'Always on My Mind' by Elvis Presley.]

⚽ 'OOH-AAH'

Reading deserve a mention for finding something useful from Gina G's Eurovision Song Contest entry 'Just a Little Bit' as they turned the song into a great piece of terrace appreciation for striker Leroy Lita.

Ooh aah, just a Lita bit
Ooh aah, a Lita bit more!
Ooh aah just a Lita bit!
Give him the ball and he will score!

[To the tune of 'Just a Little Bit' by Gina G.]

⚽ X-RATED

As we have already seen, any player with '-unt' in their name is asking for a song laced with innuendo. Hereford fans are not ones to mince their words, however, so put your hands over your kids' ears:

Posh Spice is a slapper
She has a saggy c**t
And when she's shagging Beckham
She thinks of Kenny Lunt!

[To the tune of 'My Old Man's a Dustman' by Lonnie Donegan.]

⚽ 'RED DOG'

When goalkeeper Lee Camp moved from Derby County to their arch-rivals Nottingham Forest in 2008, fans of both clubs were not amused. The Rams were angry with Camp for defecting to a club they despised and Forest were a bit miffed that a player they once hated would now have to be cheered.

So what did Camp do to win over Forest? Simple – in the dying seconds of a match against former club Derby in the 2008/09 season, the game was deadlocked at 1–1. But then County won a penalty and the chance to beat their hated enemy. Nacer Barazite steps up to win it for the Rams... Camp

saves! 'You can say the game was what dreams are made of,' the new Forest hero said afterwards. But then he ruined it by saying: 'I am a Derby boy and still live in Derby – I hope they still get promoted.' Ah, not the best way to endear you to your new fans, but Forest didn't mind and came up with this:

Lee Camp is a Red dog
He used to be a Ram
But then he signed for Forest
'Cos he's a proper man

He took the shit from Derby
And kissed the Forest tree
And then he went and took the piss
And saved their penalty!

[Again, sung to the tune of 'My Old Man's a Dustman'.]

⚽ 'SHOW US URAS'

Falkirk fans lead the way with this excellent bit of innuendo:

Cedric, show us Uras!
Cedric, Cedric, show us Uras!

[Sung to French defender Cedric Uras in 1997.]

⚽ '21 OR 28?'

Football fanatics have their own warped assumptions – especially those fans heralding from Tyneside. Apart from insisting they support a 'big' club, they are also unconvinced about Obafemi Martins' real age. Fellow Nigerian Kanu suffers from the same conspiracy theories. It's suggested that the players have lied about their ages to continue playing in the top flight for longer. True or not, it makes for a great song:

Oba, Oba-fem
Oba, Oba-fem
Oba, Oba-fem
Obafemi Martins!
21 or 28?
21 or 28?
21 or 28?
Obafemi Martins!

[To the tune of 'Skip to My Lou', a popular children's song.]

Ole Gunnar Solskjaer wrote his name into Manchester United folklore when he scored a 93rd minute winner against Bayern Munich in the 1999 Champions League final. The goal capped a stunning comeback from United, following Teddy Sheringham's

145

90th-minute equaliser against the German giants. And after Ole's goal won the match and completed United's remarkable Treble, the Norwegian striker had also earned himself a new song:

Who put the ball in the Germans' net?
Who put the ball in the Germans' net?
Who put the ball in the Germans' net?
Ole Gunnar Solskjaer!

⚽ 'WE DON'T NEED VIAGRA'

From raucous Birmingham City fans at St Andrews in 2008:

We don't need Viagra to stay up!
We don't need Viagra to stay up!
We don't need Viagra, we don't need Viagra!
We don't need Viagra to stay up!

[To the tune of 'She'll Be Coming Round the Mountain'. Birmingham were relegated that season. I'll leave you to write the 'going down' gags…]

⚽ 'EVERY SINGLE ONE OF US'

Sir Alex Ferguson was due to retire as Manchester United manager after the 2001/02 season. Thankfully for the United fans, he changed his mind

– with a little help from wife Cathy. 'It was really Cathy's idea. If she hadn't come up with it and the boys hadn't given full support, I wouldn't have considered a change of mind,' Ferguson once said. The United fans were delighted to hear about Sir Alex's U-turn and quickly drummed up some support for his wife:

Oh every single one of us
Loves Cathy Ferguson, loves Cathy Ferguson!
Oh every single one of us
Loves Cathy Ferguson, loves Cathy Ferguson!

⚽ 'FEED THE GOAT'

Shaun Goater could hardly be described as a one-club man. The Bermuda striker played for Manchester clubs City and United, along with Rotherham, Notts County, Reading, Coventry City, Southend United and the all-conquering Bermuda Hogges. He had a hit-and-miss career, much like his shooting style, but when he did manage to find form, he was rewarded with this from his adoring fans:

Feed the Goat and he will score!
Feed the Goat! Feed the Goat!
Feed the Goat and he will score!

[Sung to the tune of good old 'Bread of Heaven'.]

147

The Referee's a W****r

Fulham eulogise over towering Norwegian defender Brede Hangeland, with the same tune as 'Feed the Goat':

Brede Hangeland, Brede Hangeland
He is Norway's Bobby Moore!
He is Norway's Bobby Moore!

Another, more elaborate, tribute to the big Norwegian, heard at Fulham's match at Aston Villa in 2008/09, to the tune of Ram Jam's 'Black Betty':

Oh Big Brede (Hangeland!)
Whoa big Brede! (Hangeland!)
He jumps so high (Hangeland!)
You know that's no lie! (Hangeland!)
He's so rock steady! (Hangeland!)
When you see him on telly! (Hangeland!)
Oh Big Brede! (Hangeland!)
Whoa big Brede! (Hangeland!)

'LIVERPOOL'S NUMBER NINE'

From Brede Hangeland to Fernando Torres:

His armband proved he was a red
Torres! Torres!
You'll Never Walk Alone it said
Torres! Torres!

We bought the lad from sunny Spain
He gets the ball he scores again
Fernando Torres! Liverpool's number nine!

[To the tune of 'The Animals Went in Two by Two',
a popular children's song.]

From Torres to Aston Villa defender Carlos Cuellar:

Dee-dum, dee-dum, dee-dum, dee-dum, Car-los
Cuellar
Dee-dum, dee-dum, dee-dum, dee-dum, Car-los
Cuellar
He's 6ft 3in with curly hair, and goofy teeth but we
don't care
He's Carlos Cuellar, the Villa centre-half!

And from Cuellar to Arsenal striker Eduardo:

He came to us when Henry went
Eddie! Eddie!
He scored more goals than Darren Bent
Eddie! Eddie!
He broke his leg but he'll be back
And Darren Bent will still be cack
Eduardo Silva, Arsenal's number nine!

⚽ 'HE'S AN ENGLISHMAN AT ARSENAL'

Arsenal manager Arsène Wenger once named a team entirely made up of foreigners[*], so the fans' appreciation was clear for all to see when Theo Walcott joined them in 2006.

Oh Theo, Theo
Theo, Theo Walcott
He's an Englishman at Ar-se-nal!

[To the tune of 'Englishman in New York' by Sting.]

* The Arsenal team that beat Crystal Palace 5–1 at Highbury on 14 February 2005 was: Lehmann, Lauren, Toure, Cygan, Clichy, Pires (Fabregas 80), Vieira, Edu (Flamini 61), Reyes, Bergkamp (van Persie 79), Henry. Subs not used: Senderos, Almunia.

Aston Villa loved Dwight Yorke until he signed for Manchester United – then the hatred began. Reminding him of happier days, here's what they used to sing, again in the style of Sting's 'Englishman in New York':

When he's on the pitch at Villa Park
And he's really on his game
He can twist and turn and score a goal
Everybody knows his name!

Whoa, he's a footballer
An Aston Villa footballer
He's a footballer called Dwight Yorke!

⚽ 'ODE TO CITY GROUND'

Nottingham Forest fans haven't had much to sing about since the European Cup glory days back in the late 1970s and early 1980s, but they do manage a mention with this impressive ode to the City Ground, Forest's home:

Far have we travelled
And much have we seen
Goodison, Anfield are places we've been
Maine Road, Old Trafford still echo to the sounds
Of the boys in the Red shirts from City Ground
City Ground!
Oh mist rolling in from the Trent
My desire is always to be there
Oh City Ground!

[To the tune of 'Mull of Kintyre' by Paul McCartney.]

⚽ 'IS THAT ALL SHE GETS?'

During an FA Cup clash between Chelsea and Shrewsbury in 2003, the game was halted momentarily as a streaker charged on to the pitch.

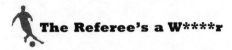

After hearing the abuse he got from the stands, the red-faced male was quickly escorted off the pitch.

Is that all she gets at home?
Is that all she, is that all she
Is that all she gets at home?

['Bread of Heaven', of course!]

⚽ 'THREE FAT GOONERS'

Following on from a song for Arsenal and one inspired by the FA Cup, here's Tottenham combining the two brilliantly, to the tune of 'Ten Green Bottles':

Three fat Gooners standing in the wall
Three fat Gooners standing in the wall
And if one Paul Gascoigne should bend it round the wall
There'll be one sick Seaman standing in the goal!

[This song was to celebrate Paul Gascoigne's 30-yard thunderbolt free-kick in the 1991 FA Cup semi-final.]

⚽ 'SEXIST ARMY'

In 2006, Mike Newell was incensed with referee Amy Rayner after she failed to give his side a penalty in a match against Queens Park Rangers.

Luton went on to lose the game 3-2 and Newell was not pleased with ref Amy's performance:

'It is tokenism – for the politically-correct idiots,' said Newell. 'We have a problem in this country with political correctness, and bringing women into the game is not the way to improve refereeing and officialdom. It is bad enough with the incapable referees and linesmen we have, but if you start bringing in women, you have big problems.'

While Newell was reprimanded for his comments, he did receive support from the Hatters fans, who adapted the classic 'Barmy Army' chant:

Mike Newell's sexist army!

⚽ 'SPEAKING WORDS OF WISDOM'

Chairmen can be very difficult to work with. The men in the boardroom are only too happy to wield the axe should results waver, but Middlesbrough supremo Steve Gibson is a different type of beast. The chairman is widely regarded as one of the most patient in the Football League and, despite Middlesbrough's relegation to the Championship, he kept faith with Gareth Southgate. The 'Boro fans love him, hence:

When we find ourselves in times of trouble
Stevie Gibson comes to me

The Referee's a W****r

Speaking words of wisdom, MFC!
MFC, MFC, MFC, MFC,
There will be an answer, MFC!

[To the tune of 'Let It Be' by the Beatles. Gibson eventually ran out of patience and sacked Southgate in October 2009.]

And before it all went wrong at Newcastle:

When we find ourselves in times of trouble
Kevin Keegan comes to me
Speaking words of wisdom
Geremi!

[Where do we start with this one? Kevin Keegan's wisdom, or Geremi being the answer? Both ideas proved wide of the mark, and Newcastle slipped down to the Championship in 2009.]

⚽ 'YOU'RE INDESTRUCTIBLE'

Wigan's Mario Melchiot:

Ma-ri-o! Always believe in your soul
You've got the power to know… you're indestructible!
Always believe in, Ma-ri-o!

[To the tune of 'Gold' by Spandau Ballet.]

West Ham striker Carlton Cole:
Carlton Cole, Cole!
Always believe in your soul
You've got the power to go
You're indestructible
Always believe in…
Carlton Cole!

⚽ 'BUY OUR CLUB'

West Ham welcomed incoming owner and biscuit baron Eggert Magnusson to Upton Park in 2006 with this amusing ditty sung to the tune of the popular TV advert for Club biscuits:

If you made a lot of money selling biscuits
Buy our club!

⚽ 'SUPER-PAV'

Roman Pavlyuchenko endured a difficult spell in his debut season in English football in 2008/09. His most notable intervention was a match-winning goal in the Carling Cup against Burnley. Despite his troubles, however, he still managed to bag a respectable 15 goals, earning him a song from the White Hart Lane faithful. And what a good one it is, too:

Supercalifragilistic Roman Pavlyuchenko

Came to us from Moscow and he's better
than Shevchenko
The only guy we know who drinks his vodka from
a kenko
Supercalifragilistic Roman Pavlyuchenko!

[Sung to the tune of 'Supercalifragilisticexpialidocious'
(impressive, I know) sung by Julie Andrews in the
film *Mary Poppins*.]

Or:

Pavlyuchenko, he's our hero!
Coming all the way from Spartak Moscow!

[To the tune of 'Captain Planet', the theme tune
from the cartoon.]

'ROBBIE FOWLER HOUSE'

Robbie Fowler has ensured he will still rake it in
when he hangs up his boots by becoming a
successful property baron. The former Liverpool
striker has built up a portfolio of over 100 houses,
including an entire street in Oldham. And when he
enjoyed a brief spell at Manchester City, this brilliant
song soon sprouted up around Eastlands:

We all live in a Robbie Fowler house!

A Robbie Fowler house, a Robbie Fowler house!
[To the tune of 'Yellow Submarine' by The Beatles.]

⚽ 'MOROCCAN ALL OVER THE WORLD'

Pure genius, Norwich fans. To the tune of Status Quo's 'Rockin' All Over the World', they saluted Moroccan Youssef Saffri with this:

Here we go, here we go, here we go
Youssef's better than Juninho
Here we go-oh!
Moroccan all over the world!

⚽ 'WE'LL TAKE MORE CARE OF YOU'

Inspired by the 1980s British Airways 'We'll take more care of you' advert, Tottenham fans brilliantly adapted the cheesy slogan to a terrace tune to salute striker Steve Archibald.

We'll take more care of you – Archibald, Archibald!

[Predictably, Arsenal supporters would retaliate with 'You're just a Scottish Jew', to reflect Archibald's nationality and allegiance to Spurs, who have a traditionally strong Jewish backing.]

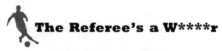

⚽ BISHOP-BASHING

It doesn't take long for fans to take make fun of a player's surname, as Bury fans show in their appreciation of star striker Andy Bishop.

You'll never bash the Bishop!

⚽ 'HE SWAM AWAY'

Time for some Culture Club now and a quite superb adaptation of 'Karma Chameleon' from the Cardiff City faithful in their appreciation of on-loan goalkeeper Dimi Konstantopoulos.

Dimi, Dimi, Dimi, Dimi, Konstantopoulos – he swam away, to Cardiff Bay!

⚽ 'SEX ON FIRE'

Temuri Ketsbaia gets another mention, this time as a manager. The arch-nemesis of the advertising boards took to management like a fish to water and, after getting Anorthosis Famagusta to the group stages of the Champions League, he became an honorary Cypriot. He also became the subject of a quite simple, but brilliant, adaptation of the Kings of Leon smash-hit 'Sex on Fire':

Whoa! Te-mu-ri Kets-baia!

[Ketsbaia resigned from the Cypriot club in April 2009 and became manager of Greek side Olympiakos. He left after only six games, despite the club winning five and drawing the other. The fans had become sick of Ketsbaia and criticised the team's playing style.]

⚽ 'IN THE MIDDLE'

Hull City goalkeeper Boaz Myhill gets his own tribute from the Tigers fans, to the tune of 'Our House' by Madness:

My-hill!
In the middle of our goal!
My-hill!

⚽ 'WE HAD JOY'

Finnish striker Jari Litmanen hardly set the place alight during his one-year spell at Liverpool in the 2001/02 season, but following his match-winning goal against Tottenham in the Premier League, the Kopites decided to think up a song for him.

It seemed to work – in the very next game after netting the winner against Spurs, Jari did it again and scored in Liverpool's 1–0 Champions League win over Dinamo Kiev.

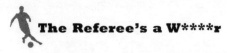

We had joy, we had fun, we've got Jari Litmanen
He's got style, he's got flair
Got a mullet, we don't care!

[To the tune of 'Seasons in the Sun', a track made famous by Terry Jacks in the 1970s and then ruined by Westlife a few decades later.]

⚽ 'WE'RE NOT ALLOWED TO SWEAR'

Cracking story, this. French defender Frank Leboeuf made an instant impact following his move to Chelsea in 1996 as the Blues fans immediately took him to their hearts. Eager to let Leboeuf know how much he was loved at Stamford Bridge, Chelsea supporters started signing: 'He's here, he's there, he's every-fucking-where, Frank Leboeuf, Frank Leboeuf.'

But Frank was not impressed. In a radio interview, he said although he was proud to have a song named after him, he was disappointed at the potty-mouthed way in which he was serenaded. 'Don't swear in my song,' was the general message. And the Chelsea faithful duly obliged:

He's here, he's there…
We're not allowed to swear!
Frank Leboeuf! Frank Leboeuf!

⚽ 'HIS NAME IS FAR TOO LONG'

When Jan Vennegoor of Hesselink joined Celtic in 2006, parents of Hoops fans must have looked at their wallets with worry. 'Mum, MUM! I want Jan Vennegoor of Hesselink on my shirt, PLEASE!' 'Son, can't you just have Bobo Balde?' Here's a Parkhead tribute to the Dutchman:

He's big
He's strong
His name is far too long
Vennegoor of Hesselink!

⚽ 'BETTER THAN ZIDANE'

Heard while at a match between Northern Ireland and San Marino in 2008:

He tackles and he passes
Hassles and harasses
He gets up peoples arses
He's better than Zidane!
Der-der-der-der... Grant McCann!

[To the tune of the *Addams Family* theme tune.]
More *Addams Family* fun...

In our defensive foursome

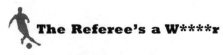

The Referee's a W****r

He's absolutely awesome
From corners he will score some
It's Ugo Ehiogu!
Der-der-der-der… Ugo!

⚽ 'HIS DAD OWNS A CHIPPY'

Clearly forgetting that not all Chinese men own a takeaway shop, Manchester City fans loved to sing this about defender Sun Jihai:

Singing aye-yi-yippee Sun Jihai!
Singing aye-yi-yippee Sun Jihai!
Singing aye-yi-yippee, his dad owns a chippy!
Aye-yi-yippee Sun Jihai!

[To the tune of 'She'll Be Coming Round the Mountain'.]

⚽ MICHAEL OWEN

The shock summer story of 2009 was undoubtedly Michael Owen's free transfer to Manchester United. Owen became a laughing stock when his management team created a brochure advertising his skills. Words such as 'cool', 'young' and 'sincere' were used to describe the former Liverpool striker. Strangely, 'injury prone' was omitted amid a barrage of gushing PR nonsense.

Some United fans were outraged to see Owen, with his Merseyside connections, join the club, but Old Trafford eventually warmed to him and created an impressive tribute, while at the same time pouring scorn on their Scouse enemies:

Ow, Ow, Owen's on
Give the lad the ball
He'll stick it in the dippers' net
And they will win fuck-all!

[To the tune of 'Row, Row, Row Your Boat'. Dippers, in case you're wondering, is the affectionate term used by Mancunians to refer to their bitter rivals along the East Lancs Road. The term plays on the stereotype that Merseyside is a deprived area and that the inhabitants of the city are so desperate for food, they would dip into bins to find something to eat.]

Next up, it's time to dip into 'Doing the 92'...

CHAPTER FOUR: DOING THE 92

Although you'll have become accustomed to singing songs about porn and tiny Cox, please don't get ahead of yourselves at the mention of 'Doing the 92'.

The phrase refers to the hardy souls who have travelled the length and breadth of Great Britain in a bid to visit every single one of the 92 teams in the Football League. These heroes had the guts to go the extra mile – literally – but they didn't have a song to accompany them at every ground.

So if you're man/mad enough to take on the challenge, let's start at A.

⚽ ACCRINGTON STANLEY

You light up my senses, like a gallon of Magnet
Like a packet of Woodbines, like a good pinch of snuff
Like a night out in Accy

The Referee's a W****r

Like a greasy chip butty
Oh Accrington Stanley
Come fill me again...
Na na na na na na, ooh!

[To the tune of 'Annie's Song' by John Denver. This song is widely renowned as the 'Greasy Chip Butty Song' and Sheffield United supporters are generally recognised as the ones who started it. The length, tune and misty-eyed affection for the town and the football team make it an anthem not just at 'Accy' but across the globe. Even Canadian side Toronto FC have their own version!]

⚽ AFC BOURNEMOUTH

Sea, sea
Sea-si-ders!

[Simple and effective from the Cherries fans.]

⚽ ALDERSHOT

The Shots are one of many teams that hijack the 'Vindaloo' song by Fat Les, which involves humming the tune and then replacing the original yell of 'England' with their team's name, in this case, 'The Shots'. A more imaginative tune heard on the terraces at The Rec is:

Everywhere we go (Everywhere we go)
People want to know (People want to know)
Who we are (Who we are)
Shall we tell 'em? (Shall we tell 'em?)
We are the Aldershot, (We are the Aldershot)
Play in red and blue (Play in red and blue)
We hate the Farnborough (We hate the Farnborough)
We hate the Reading (We hate the Reading)
Who are we? (Who are we?)
The Aldershot, The Aldershot...

[Scout tune, unknown.]

⚽ ARSENAL

The ubiquitous 'One-nil to the Ar-sen-al' has followed the Gunners around ever since the George Graham era from 1986–1995. Graham's men were renowned for eking out 1–0 wins and fans would herald the side's success with this tribute:

One-nil, to the Ar-se-nal!
One-nil, to the Ar-sen-al!
One-nil, to the Ar-sen-al!!

⚽ ASTON VILLA

While the chant – which increases in volume with every passing word – 'Villa, Villa, Villa' is the most

audible on match days at Villa Park, the Holte End masses warm up for the simple song with a long-winded attack on bitter Midlands rivals Birmingham City.

As I walked on to the steps of the Holte End
As I walked on to the Holte End one day
I saw a young Bluenose all cut up in ribbons
Battered and bleeding on the Holte End he lay

I said to the Bluenose what has happened to you
Why have they beat you and left you this way
He said all I did was to come on the Holte End
To come on the Holte End to sing and to pray

I sang that the City were better than Villa
That Villa were shit and they couldn't play
So they beat me and cut me and left me in ribbons
And here in a pool of my own blood I lay

So let this be a lesson to all Bluenosed bastards
Don't come on the Holte End to sing and to pray
'Cause if you dare say a word about our Aston Villa
It'll be the last fucking word that you'll ever say.
Villa, Villa, Villa, Villa!

⚽ BARNET

While the usual generic songs are heard at

Underhill, get yourself down there for the festive period and do your best Bing Crosby impression:

I'm dreaming of a nine-point Christmas
Just like the ones I used to know
Where the goalposts glistened
And children listened
To hear the West Bank in full flow (in full flow)

[To the tune of 'White Christmas'. A nine-point Christmas refers to the importance of winning the three games across the festive period. Usually these are 23 and 26 December and New Year's Day. Getting nine points from those fixtures can make or break a season.]

⚽ BARNSLEY

Barnsley are one of the many teams to adopt the catchy 'Ring of Fire' song and hum it on their travels or at Oakwell. But, thanks to one man, the Tykes have a new anthem.

On 17 February 2009, Jamal Campbell-Ryce netted what turned out to be the only goal of the game away at Barnsley's bitter rivals Sheffield Wednesday – yet he is not the hero. A place in Barnsley folklore is reserved for defender Bobby Hassell, whose miraculous goal line clearance in the final minute meant the visitors completed the

double over Wednesday for the first time in 63 years.

There's only one Bobby Hassell!
One Bobby Hassell!
Walking along, singing a song
Walking in a Hassell wonderland!

⚽ BIRMINGHAM CITY

While Birmingham fans are keen to fantasise about killing Aston Villa fans, this one is much less offensive, but just as good to hear in full flow:

Hark now hear the City sing
The Villa ran away
And we will sing forever more
Because of derby day!

[To the tune of 'Mary's Boy Child'. Many other supporters have adopted this as their own, usually to voice their dislike for their team's nearest rivals.]

⚽ BLACKBURN ROVERS

To claim that Blackburn Rovers and Burnley fans don't get on is a little like saying that Muhammad Ali's celebrated Rumble in the Jungle fight with George Foreman was nothing more than a scuffle.

The two sets of fans have anthems attacking one another, starting with Rovers' version of 'No Nay Never', to the tune of 'Wild Rover', the popular folk song.

There's an ale house in Burnley I used to frequent
I met Stevie Cotterill
His money was spent
He asked me to play
I answered him nay
'Cos I'll hate Burnley bastards till my dying day

Chorus:
And it's no nay never
No nay never no more
Till we play Burnley bastards
No nay never no more

I showed him a trophy so shiny and bright
And Stevie's eyes opened up with delight
I told him, 'We've won leagues and cups of the best
I'll take you down Ewood and show you the rest

[chorus]

He went back to Burnley, confessed what he'd done
And asked them to pardon their prodigal son
But Burnley's 5,000 are 'packed' in Turf Moor
They'll still tell you they had 10,000 more

The Referee's a W****r

[chorus]

I've followed the Rovers for many a year
And I've spent all my money on tickets and beer
Still Burnley's 5,000 are slumped in the turf
They'll tell you that they're the best fans on the earth

[chorus]

[A more family-friendly version is played out over the Tannoy system when the players run out at Ewood Park. The song is in response to Burnley's version proclaiming their desire to play Blackburn again and beat them. The Clarets lived perennially in the shadow of Rovers, who won the Premier League title in 1995 while Burnley were relegated from Division One. Burnley finally got their wish in December 2000 as the teams met for the first time in 18 years. Rovers won the Division One match 2–0 and then 5–0 in April 2001.]

⚽ BLACKPOOL

Like Bournemouth, Blackpool's rendition of 'Sea, sea, sea-siders' gets the most airtime at Bloomfield Road.

⚽ BOLTON

The Wanderers moved to the Reebok Stadium in

1997, ending their 102-year stay at Burnden Park. They may have moved to a state-of-the-art modern stadium, but Bolton fans still pay tribute to their former home.

Oh my lads you should have seen 'em running
Asked them why and they replied, the Bolton boys are coming
All the lads and lasses, smiles upon their faces
Walkin' down the Manny Road to see the Burnden aces!

['Manny Road' refers to Manchester Road, which was adjacent to Burnden Park.]

⚽ BRADFORD CITY

Take me home, Midland Road
To the place I belong!
To the Valley
To see the City
Take me home, Midland Road!

[To the tune of 'Take Me Home, Country Roads' by John Denver.]

⚽ BRENTFORD

Griffin Park can hardly be described as rocking at

the best of times. Here's Sam Wood, a rising star in west London: 'I can't really remember many songs the fans sing. They sing "Charlie! Charlie!" for Charlie McDonald, but that's as much as I know. That's about as thoughtful as we get!'

As well as that very imaginative ode to McDonald (which somehow didn't get into the 'Heroes' section – I wonder why?) the Bees fans also adopt the Beatles' 'Hey Jude' and sing:

La, la la la la la la
La la la la
Brentford!

Yawn.

⚽ BRIGHTON AND HOVE ALBION

When Seagulls fans aren't singing about maiming the Eagles at Crystal Palace, the crowd at the Withdean likes to reminisce about more successful times:

Good old Sussex by the sea
Good old Sussex by the sea
We're going up
To win the Cup
For Sussex by the sea!

[To the tune of 'Sussex by the Sea,' a song by

William Ward-Higgs. Brighton held Manchester
United to a 2–2 draw in the 1983 FA Cup final, but
after losing the replay 4–0, things went from bad to
worse for the Sussex club. They flirted with
bankruptcy and almost dropped out of the Football
League in 1997 and, with the team currently in
League One, the fans sing this to remind themselves
of brighter times.]

And then there's all those homophobic comebacks –
check out 'Funnies' for those.

⚽ BRISTOL CITY

The Wurzels love Bristol City and released the song
'One for the Bristol City' in 1976, but a lesser-known
hit, 'Drink Up Thy Zider', has been reworked into a
classic anthem sung at Ashton Gate:

Drink Up Thy Zider, Drink Up Thy Zider
For tonight we'll merry be, merry be!
We'll knock their milk churns over (We're going
down the Rovers)
Then roll 'em in the clover (To do the bastards over)
There's still more Zider in the jar!

[To the tune of 'Drink Up Thy Zider' by the Wurzels.]

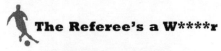

🅑 BRISTOL ROVERS

Leadbelly's 'Goodnight Irene' is a fan favourite with Rovers – although the origins of the song remain unclear. Some Rovers supporters say it started in the 1950s when a version of the song was in the charts. One of the lines in the song included the words 'sometimes I have a great notion to jump in the river and drown'.

The Bristol Frome flows alongside Rovers' old Eastville ground and, when the team lost, the line about jumping into the river seemed to fit.

Irene goodnight, Irene goodnight
Goodnight Irene, goodnight Irene
I'll see you in my dreams!

🅑 BURNLEY

Burnley stepped up the verbal jousting with rivals Blackburn Rovers with their version of 'No Nay Never' and the anthem will be heard loud and clear throughout the 2009/10 season as Owen Coyle's men taste top-flight football for the first time in 33 years. When Rovers come to town, you can expect a rousing rendition of:

I went to the alehouse I often frequent
I saw old Jack Walker his money was spent

He asked me to play
I answered him nay
With rubbish like yours I can beat any day

Chorus:
And it's no nay never
No nay never no more
Till we play bastard Rovers
No never no more

Ewood's now empty, it's getting knocked down
They play their home games on a piece of waste ground
Jack Walker looks round and says something's not right
'Cos there's far more players than supporters in sight

[chorus]

Five years have now passed and Burnley rule supreme
The league and the cup have been won by our team
The bastards are bankrupt and long since have died
And Jack Walker sweeps up down at Burnley's long side.

⚽ BURTON ALBION

You fill up my senses
Like a gallon of Peddi

The Referee's a W****r

Like a packet of Walkers
Like a good pinch of snuff
Like a night out in Burton
Like a greasy chip butty
Like Burton Albion
Come fill me again...
Na na na na na na, ooh!

['The Greasy Chip Butty' song crops up again here. The 'Peddi' refers to Marston's Pedigree, a beer brewed in Burton. 'Walkers' refers to the crisps.]

⚽ BURY

Andy Bishop bangs 'em in for fun at Bury and his goals have earned him a place in the fans' hearts as well as their hymn sheets. While the usual 'Stand up if you love Bury' chants can be heard at Gigg Lane, the ode to Bishop is always audible.

Do-do-do-do!
Andy Bishop!
Do-do-do-do!
Andy Bishop!

[To the tune of Perfecto Allstars' 'Reach Up (Papa's Got A Brand New Pigbag)'.]

⚽ CARDIFF CITY

Check the 'Hero Worship' chapter and you'll see that Cardiff's song for Kasper 'The Friendly Ghost' Schmeichel will take some beating. The Welsh club also manage to raise a smile with their tongue-in-cheek appreciation for Steve McClaren:

One Steve McClaren!
There's only one Steve McClaren!
One Steve McClaren!
There's only one Steve McClaren!

[McClaren ruined England's summer in 2008 when he failed in his Euro 2008 qualifying bid while in charge of the England team. Clearly this was excellent news for everyone in Wales.]

⚽ CARLISLE

On 20 February 1993 Bury beat Carlisle 6–0, but the beleaguered Carlisle fans deserve credit for keeping up their spirits with a great piece of gallows humour:

We'll score again – don't know where, don't know when
But I know we'll score again
Some sunny day!

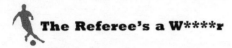
The Referee's a W****r

[Adapted from 'We'll Meet Again' by Vera Lynn. Asking for a sunny day in a match between Bury and Carlisle is wishful thinking pushed to the limits, but you can't fault Carlisle for their optimism. The song has since caught on and become a mainstay at Brunton Park.]

⚽ CHARLTON

Charlton run out to 'Red, Red Robin' by Bill Cotton and, although the song gets decent coverage at the Valley, the fans' favourite remains 'Valley, Floyd Road', to the tune of Paul McCartney's 'Mull of Kintyre'. Floyd Road refers to the address of Charlton's stadium.

Chorus:
Valley, Floyd Road
The mist rolling in from the Thames
My desire is always to be found at
Valley, Floyd Road
Many miles have I travelled
Many games have I seen
Following Charlton my favourite team
Many hours have I spent in the covered end choir
Singing Valley, Floyd Road
My only desire

[chorus]

From Selhurst to West Ham
Many years did we roam
Forever dreaming of returning home
To follow our team every year we aspired
Singing Valley, Floyd Road
In the covered end choir

[chorus]

The fifth of December 1992,
The exile is over, our dreams have come true
Charlton at home, there's no more I require
Singing Valley, Floyd Road
My only desire

[chorus]

Many miles have I travelled
Many games have I seen
Following Charlton my favourite team
Many hours have I spent in the covered end choir
Singing Valley, Floyd Road
My only desire.

[chorus]

[The line 'fifth of December 1992' refers to the date
when Charlton returned to The Valley, following
the end of their seven-year groundshare with

Crystal Palace. Charlton beat Portsmouth 1–0 courtesy of a Colin Walsh goal and lifelong Addicks fan Richard Hunt, who helped engineer the move back to SE7, said: 'It was the unique noise of a crowd sweeping away seven years of pain and celebrating the right to do something ordinary again – watch football at Charlton – as a result of an extraordinary collective achievement. The goal was the moment at which I started to shed my tears, but everyone was celebrating. We had cried, ached, shouted, cajoled, lobbied and, most of all, dreamed of these 90 minutes.'

The Addicks also deserve a quick mention for their predictable-yet-funny tribute to Andy Hunt... go to 'Hero Worship' for that one.]

⚽ CHELSEA

Bovril, beers, meat pies and sausage rolls represent a great staple diet for the typical football fan, but just try telling that to followers of Chelsea. The West Londoners have been taking celery to the stands for well over 20 years, all the while singing:

Celery! Celery!
If she don't come, I'll tickle her bum...
With a stick of celery!

[The curious exercise began in the 1980s when

Chelsea were so poor, fans resorted to chucking the crunchy foodstuff at each other and on to the pitch as a way of bringing some light to their otherwise gloomy outlook.

This Chelsea anthem has charmed its way into Blues' songbooks, but fans have been warned not to take the vegetable with them to matches following instances of celery-induced violence.

Take Chelsea's FA Cup semi-final clash with Fulham in 2002, for instance. Charlie Driver, 40, David Blake, 28, and Robbie Sanders, 28, were all given good behaviour orders by Birmingham magistrates after they threw celery sticks in the direction of then Fulham manager Jean Tigana. But given the fact a type of facial mutilation is named after the Chelsea, celery-throwing could be seen as a step forward.

The 'Chelsea Three' were warned they would be fined £300 if they were caught throwing the stuff again, leaving Mr Driver to say: 'I am relieved I can still watch Chelsea, but I won't be eating celery anymore, or throwing it.' Mrs Driver will be disappointed.]

⚽ CHELTENHAM TOWN

Que sera, sera
Whatever will be, will be
We're going to Shrews-bu-ry
Que sera, sera!

The Referee's a W****r

[Credit to the Cheltenham fans for seeing the funny side of their plight in the 2008/09 season. With relegation from League One still undecided, the supporters clearly knew the game was up and matches with Shrewsbury in League Two were only a few months away.]

⚽ CHESTERFIELD

You're not a true romantic if you don't remember the Spireites' FA Cup run in 1997. John Duncan's lowly team, languishing in the third tier of English football, made it to the semi-finals of the Cup before that incredible 3–3 draw against Premier League side Middlesbrough.

The referee (who'd have thought it?) turned out to be the villain, crushing Chesterfield's hopes of an FA Cup final appearance. Jon Howard's shot crashed off the bar – and over the line – but David Elleray did not give the goal. It finished 3–3 and Chesterfield lost the replay 3–0. Never has 'The referee's a wanker' seemed more appropriate.

If Chesterfield's sensational run in the cup came as a surprise, the fact that their anthem for the world's greatest knockout competition outsold the Spice Girls was anything but. The brilliant 'We Can Build Our Dreams', a collaboration between the football club and local band Kaught in the Akt, is sung fondly by the Chesterfield faithful as they reminisce about that glorious run. 'I do have a copy of that,' admitted Duncan. 'And it outsold the Spice Girls – in Derbyshire at least! But we knew this would be a once-in-a-lifetime thing, so we thought we should do everything we can for the cup. We decided to embrace it, not to fight it.'

⚽ COLCHESTER UNITED

Oh when the Us
(Oh when the Us)
Go steaming in
(Go steaming in)
Oh when the Us go steaming in
I wanna be in that number
Oh when the Us go steaming in!

[Nice variation on 'When the Saints Go Marching In' from the United fans here.]

⚽ COVENTRY CITY

Coventry's success on the pitch in recent years has been sporadic at best but their fans are at the top of the league when it comes to self-deprecation.

In our Coventry homes, in our Coventry homes!
We speak with an accent ex-cee-ding-ly rare
You want a cathedral, we've got one to spare

The Referee's a W****r

In our Coventry homes!

[Just brilliant. The tune is sung in the same way fans sing 'In Your Liverpool Slums' when the Merseysiders come to town.]

⚽ CREWE ALEXANDRA

'Que sera, sera' gets another outing here:

When I was just a little boy
I asked my mother what should I be
Should I be Vale? Should I be Stoke?
Here's what she said to me:
Wash your mouth out son
And fetch your father's gun!
And shoot the clayhead scum!
Shoot the clayhead scum!

['Clayhead' is a slang term to denote someone heralding from the city of Stoke – a place also known as the Potteries.]

⚽ CRYSTAL PALACE

Anyone at Selhurst Park on match days will normally hear the 'Olé olé olé' chant with 'Eagles!' added on to the end, or the excellent Vic Moses appreciation, but you're not a fully-fledged Eagle

until you belt out 'Glad All Over' by the Dave Clark Five.

⚽ DAGENHAM AND REDBRIDGE

The Essex club are usually slated by opposition supporters for being a pub team, hence the Daggers' humorous retort:

Pub team from Essex!
We're just a pub team from Essex!
Pub team from Essex! We're just a pub team from Essex!

[More 'Guantanamera'.]

⚽ DARLINGTON

Preparing for a wet Wednesday night in Darlington isn't the most glamorous of scenarios. The home fans are always quick to point out the lack of away support at the Darlington Arena and their own version of 'Guantanamera' has been adopted by many northern teams:

Come in a taxi! You should've come in a taxi!
Come in a taxi! You should've come in a taxi!

[Usually sung to the travelling hordes, or lack of them.]

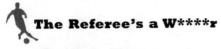

⚽ DERBY COUNTY

Noting the numerous chants about hated rivals Nottingham Forest would be far too easy and unimaginative and, in any case, nothing will ever beat the song from the delirious Rams in the away section at Old Trafford in 1997.

The telescopic-legged Costa Rican Paulo Wanchope led the United defenders a merry dance and brilliantly slotted the ball past Peter Schmeichel as Derby shocked United 3–2. His goal was later voted the best in Derby's history by fans, as part of their 125th anniversary celebrations. The chant was just as good. Remember – it's all about simplicity.

There's only Wan-chope!

⚽ DONCASTER ROVERS

In Dublin's fair city, where girls are so pretty
That's where I first set my eyes on Sweet Molly Malone
She wheeled her wheelbarrow
Through streets broad and narrow
Singing (clap, clap) Rovers!

[To the tune of 'Molly Malone', an Irish classic.]

⚽ EVERTON

When the Toffees are not humming along to *Z-Cars*, they have some amusing tributes in their repertoire. The Leighton Baines appreciation is a tasty little number and can be found in the 'Heroes' section. For an altogether more intimidating rally-cry, 'The Banks of the Royal Blue Mersey' is the anthem of choice, but that's dealt with in the 'X-Rated' section. In the meantime:

It's a grand old team to play for
And it's a grand old team to support
And if you know your history
It's enough to make your heart go whoa!
We don't care what the Reds' fans say
What the heck should we care
Because we only know
That if there's gonna be a show
Then the Everton boys will be there
Everton! (repeat with clapping)

⚽ EXETER CITY

It's not often League One side Exeter can be mentioned in the same breath as Manchester United and Liverpool, but their chant for striker Adam Stansfield is sung to the same tune as Liverpool's 'Number Nine' for Fernando Torres and United's

'When Johnny Goes Marching' ode to defender John O'Shea.

He is a Grecian through and through
Stano! Stano!
He is a Grecian through and through
Stano! Stano!
We brought the lad from He-re-ford
Give him the ball, he'll score for us
Ad-am Stans-field City's number nine!

[The Grecians are not the only admirers of Mr Stansfield. *Soccer Saturday* supremo Jeff Stelling jokes whenever he scores that 'sister Lisa will be happy', meaning Lisa Stansfield, the singer. The pair are not related.]

⚽ FULHAM

Fulham's collection of tributes, like their squad, lacks depth. Aside from the generic 'We love you Fulham, we do' or 'If you all hate Chelsea clap yer hands', there is one comedy gem:

Al-Fayed, Whoa!
Al-Fayed, Whoa!
He wants to be a Brit!
And QPR are shit!

[Some Anglo-Saxon language from the normally mild-mannered Cottagers fans. Check the 'Heroes' section for the tune, referring to the club's owner and Harrods number one Mohammed Al-Fayed.]

⚽ GILLINGHAM

The Beatles' 'Hey Jude' provides the tune for the Gills fans' favourite, sung primarily at the Rainham End of the Priestfield Stadium when the game is drawing to a close.

The last waltz with you
Two lonely people together I fell in love with you
The last waltz will last forever
It's all over now
Nothing left to say just the Gills and the Rainham End singing:
La, la la la la la la! La la la la!
The Gills!
La, la la la la la la! La la la la!
The Gills!

⚽ GRIMSBY TOWN

Top marks for the Mariners here. The chant started up whenever the England rugby team were playing (to the tune of 'Swing Low, Sweet Chariot'), but it

has became so popular among fans it is now an ever-present at Blundell Park.

Swing low, sweet ha-li-but!

[Fantastic! Grimsby is a renowned fishing town, home of Young's fishmongers.]

⚽ HARTLEPOOL UNITED

Pool still like to annoy everyone with their rendition of Rolf Harris's 'Two Little Boys', but whenever James Brown scores, expect the supporters to do their best James Brown impression, with a resounding chorus of 'I Got You (I Feel Good)'.

⚽ HEREFORD UNITED

The late, great Danny Lee penned United's anthem 'We All Love You' in the 1970s and every match, home or away, the fans will sing the song to celebrate and remember the tireless fundraiser and supreme entertainer, who used to walk around the perimeter at Edgar Street while balancing a pint glass on his head!

Hereford United we all love you
We'll always support you and we'll follow you, too

⚽ HUDDERSFIELD TOWN

Aside from the usual proclamations of 'There's only one team in Yorkshire', the Terriers have this anthem that rips off the Sex Pistols:

I am a Hudders fan
I am a Yorkshire man
I know what I want and I know how to get it
I wanna destroy Bradford and Leeds
'Cos I wanna be... HTFC!

[To the tune of 'Anarchy in the UK'.]

⚽ HULL CITY

In the early stages of the 2008/09 season, new boys Hull City had the audacity to be dreaming of European qualification. Following wins at Newcastle, Tottenham and Arsenal, Phil Brown's Tigers had the Premier League running scared. And then came their downfall. On Boxing Day 2008, Hull were 4–0 down at Manchester City at half-time. Instead of the usual pep-talk in the dressing-room, however, Brown made an example of his players on the pitch, right in front of the disbelieving Hull fans. It didn't seem to do the trick – Hull went on to lose 5–1 and slipped into an alarming freefall from then on – they won once in 19 league games and went

into the final day of the season with relegation very much a certainty.

Champions Manchester United beat the Tigers 1–0 at the KC Stadium, but Newcastle's inability to get a draw at Aston Villa meant Brown had saved himself. The perma-tanned Hull supremo was clearly ecstatic as he grabbed the nearest microphone to murder the club's anthem:

Don't wanna go home!
Don't wanna go ho-o-o-me!
This is the best trip I've ever been on!

[To the tune of 'Sloop John B' by the Beach Boys. Brown's 'performance' was almost as embarrassing as Delia Smith's 'Let's be 'avin you' rally-cry to Norwich City fans in February 2005. The Canaries were drawing 2–2 with Manchester City at half-time, when majority shareholder Delia stumbled out on to the pitch and yelled: 'A message for the best football supporters in the world: we need a 12th man here. Where are you? Where are you? Let's be having you! Come on!' Predictably, Norwich went on to lose 3–2.

It's close, but Smith just edges it in the cringeworthy stakes. Even so, Hull City's Nicky Barmby was thoroughly unimpressed with Brown's attempts at rousing his audience and the midfielder was intent on keeping his boss firmly on the leash following Hull's 'Great Escape'. 'We'll be going out for a few beers to celebrate, but there's no way we're letting the boss near a karaoke bar,' said the former England international.]

⚽ IPSWICH TOWN

In 2006, Labour MP Ian Gibson apologised after saying inbreeding may have been to blame for a rise in cases of diabetes in his Norfolk constituency, which brings us nicely on to this ditty from Ipswich fans:

Your sister is your mother
Your father is your brother
You all shag one another... The Norwich family!

[To the *Addams Family* theme tune.]

⚽ LEEDS UNITED

As you can see, club anthems are usually born from existing songs or theme tunes, giving the fans something to manipulate into their own personal chant. Leeds United buck the trend with 'Marching on Together', which is an original composition by Les Reed and Barry Mason. The song appeared on the B-side of the Leeds United FA Cup final record, released in 1972. The vocals on the original were sung by the FA Cup finalists themselves and the club's fans. The record enjoyed a good spell in the

UK charts, peaking at number 10. What Leeds would do for similar success on the pitch…

Here we go with Leeds United
We're gonna give the boys a hand
Stand up and sing for Leeds United
They are the greatest in the land
Every day, we're all gonna say
We love you Leeds! Leeds! Leeds!
Everywhere, we're gonna be there
We love you Leeds! Leeds! Leeds!

Chorus:
Marching on together
We're gonna see you win (na na na na na na)
We are so proud
We shout it out loud
We love you Leeds! Leeds! Leeds!
We've been through it all together
And we've had our ups and downs (ups and downs!)
We're gonna stay with you forever
At least until the world stops going 'round
Every day, we're all gonna say
We love you Leeds! Leeds! Leeds!
Everywhere, we're gonna be there
We love you Leeds! Leeds! Leeds!

[chorus]

⚽ LEICESTER CITY

The anthem of choice among hardcore Foxes fans is sung to the tune of Billy Joel's 'We Didn't Start the Fire' and although it's a little too long to be remembered word-for-word, certain verses and the impressive chorus make it worthy of its status as a Walkers Stadium classic:

Lineker playing fair, Walshy here, there, everywhere
Bruno N'Gotty, Tony Cottee, super Tim Flowers

Heroes in blue and white
When I feel depressed, think of the City crest
They'll not give up the fight
Foxes never quit, you can be sure of it!

[Leicester are right – Gary Lineker certainly did play fair. In his 16 years as a professional, he was never booked. Not even once.]

⚽ LEYTON ORIENT

Simon Church enjoyed a relatively successful loan spell in the 2008/09 season with Orient and, although he didn't do enough to earn a permanent deal, he did manage to get his name sung on the terraces.

Church! Whoa! Church! Whoa!

The Referee's a W****r

His name suggests he's holy!
He's gonna beat your goalie!

⚽ LINCOLN CITY

Nice and simple from Lincoln, who rip off UB40,
who in-turn ripped off Elvis Presley:

Take my hand
Take my whole life too
'Cos I can't help falling in love with you!
Lincoln! (clap, clap, clap) Lincoln! (clap, clap, clap)

[To the tune of 'I Can't Help Falling in Love
With You'.]

⚽ LIVERPOOL

Of course the most famous Liverpool song is 'You'll
Never Walk Alone', which is in fact a show tune
from the Rodgers and Hammerstein musical
Carousel. You're not a Liverpool fan unless you can
belt that one out with the rest of the Kop. But here's
a lesser-known Anfield tune, 'Fields of Anfield
Road', a tribute to the Liverpool teams of old:

Outside the Shankly Gates
I heard a Kopite calling:
'Shankly, they have taken you away'

But you left the great eleven
Just before they took you to heaven
And the Redmen are still playing the same way

Chorus:
All round the fields of Anfield Road
Where once we watched the king Kenny play
We had Heighway on the wing
We had dreams and songs to sing
Of the glory round the fields of Anfield Road

Outside the Paisley Gates
I heard a Kopite calling:
'Paisley, they have taken you away'
But you led the great eleven
Back in Rome in seventy-seven
And the Redmen are still playing the same way

[chorus]

⚽ MACCLESFIELD

Predictable from the fans of the team they call the Silkmen:

We love our silk
(We love our silk)
In Macclesfield
(In Macclesfield)

The Referee's a W****r

We love our silk in Macclesfield
We'll show the world what were made of!
We're made of silk in Macclesfield!

[Macclesfield was once one of the largest producers
of silk in the world, hence the song.]

⚽ MANCHESTER CITY

Much in the same way that Liverpool fans need to
know 'You'll Never Walk Alone' off by heart, you
can't be considered a true Sky Blue unless you can
sing 'Blue Moon', a ballad by Lorenz Hart and
Richard Rodgers. Elvis Presley and Frank Sinatra
have covered it.

⚽ MANCHESTER UNITED

United are a force to be reckoned with off the pitch
as well as on it. They have an army of followers,
from Manchester to Moldova, and an extensive song
list to go with it. 'Glory, Glory Man United' is
universally recognised by the United faithful, but
remembering this song will earn you kudos in the
Stretford End:

Oh, me lads,
You should have seen us coming
Fastest team in the League

Just to see us running
All the lads and lasses
With smiles upon their faces
Walking down the Warwick Road!
To see Matt Busby's aces!

[To the tune of 'Blaydon Races', a Geordie folk song. Old Trafford lies at the end of Sir Matt Busby Way, which was previously called Warwick Road.]

⚽ MIDDLESBROUGH

Finding an anti-Newcastle or Sunderland song for the Boro masses to sing is far too easy – a throwback to the Ayresome Park days is a much better (and cleaner) way to announce your love of the team on match-days.

Hello, hello, we are the Boro boys
Hello, hello, we are the Boro boys
We're the Ayresome angels and we never miss a match
We all follow the Boro!

⚽ MILLWALL

Ah, Millwall. The club from South Bermondsey has been synonymous with violence and hooliganism, as this very brief timeline adequately shows:

The Referee's a W****r

FA Cup clash with Ipswich in 1978 – fighting in the stadium, coach containing Ipswich fans hit with rocks, brawls spilled out on to pitch. The Den was closed for two weeks and banned from hosting FA Cup matches for two years.

First Division play-off defeat to Birmingham in 2002 – brawl and bottle throwing – 50 policemen injures following Stern John's 90th minute winner. Then chairman Theo Paphitis: 'Once again, the thuggish element that sees football as a cover for their violent tendencies has sullied the name of football and Millwall, and brought deep distress to our local community with whom we have close ties. We also wish to express our sympathy to those police officers and horses injured.'

FA Cup clash with Hull City in 2009 – trouble on the terraces at the KC Stadium, seats thrown on to the pitch. Hull suggested Millwall 'arrived with the single intention of causing maximum disruption'. Millwall pledged to 'rid this club of the element that caused problems' in a statement of their own.

Carling Cup clash with West Ham in August 2009 – a man stabbed in the chest, riots inside and outside Upton Park – which resulted in the match being suspended – and 'deliberate and planned' brawls on the streets in east London.

As a result, the anthem of choice among the Lions' fans advocates the feeling of a siege mentality:

No one likes us! No one likes us! No one likes us – we don't care!
We are Millwall, fucking Millwall, we are Millwall – from The Den!

⚽ MK DONS

Beaten by the franchise! You're getting beaten by the franchise!

[Sung by the Dons fans, mocking their move to Milton Keynes following the financial mis-management of Wimbledon, as they were once called.]

⚽ MORECAMBE

Wise work from Morecambe fans, who sing the classic 'Bring Me Sunshine'. Which was, of course, Morecambe and Wise's signature tune.

⚽ NEWCASTLE UNITED

Former Sunderland manager Peter Reid is the subject of much vitriol on Tyneside and the Toon fans' hatred for him is summed up quite hilariously:

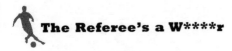

The Referee's a W****r

In the land, where I was born
Lives a man, with a monkey's head
And he went to Sunderland
And his name is Peter Reid
Altogether now!
Peter Reid's got a fucking monkey's head!
A fucking monkey's head!
A fucking monkey's head!
Peter Reid's got a fucking monkey's head!
A fucking monkey's head!
A fucking monkey's head!

[To the tune of 'Yellow Submarine' by The Beatles.]

⚽ NORTHAMPTON TOWN

More inter-city rivalry here, with the Cobblers voicing their disgust for all things Peterborough by hijacking 'London Bridge is Falling Down':

London Road is burning down
Burning down, burning down
London Road is burning down
Poor old Boro
Build it up with claret and white
Claret and white, claret and white
Build it up with claret and white
Good old Cobblers!

[London Road is Peterborough's home ground.]

⚽ NORWICH CITY

Time for a history lesson. The Canaries' anthem of choice is 'On the Ball, City', a song that is widely regarded as one of the world's oldest football songs – and it is still in use today. The chant was originally penned for Caley's FC in the 1890s before Norwich adopted it. The full version has died down, but the fans still sing the chorus at Carrow Road and on their travels. It's quite refreshing to see the innocence of the good old days rather than today's all-too-familiar attacks on Ipswich fans.

Kick it off, throw it in
Have a little scrimmage
Keep it low, splendid rush
Bravo, win or die!
On the ball City!
Never mind the danger,
Steady on, now's your chance,
Hurrah we've scored a goal!
City! (clap clap) City!

⚽ NOTTINGHAM FOREST

When the Forest faithful aren't banging on about Derby County supporters and their unhealthy fascination with sheep, they – for reasons known

only to themselves – like to break into a rendition of 'You've Lost That Lovin' Feelin'' by the Righteous Brothers, especially when they've taken the lead.

⚽ NOTTS COUNTY

Anyone lucky enough to go down to Meadow Lane will have undoubtedly left with one main question in their heads: 'Why the hell were they singing about wheelbarrows?' The chant is as follows:

I had a wheelbarrow, the wheel fell off
I had a wheelbarrow, the wheel fell off!

[To the tune 'On Top of Old Smokey', an American folk song. County were 2–0 down away at Shrewsbury in 1990 and with the team staring the ignominy of defeat square in the face, the mood at New Meadow was low. The jubilant Shrews fans were in good voice, but the visiting supporters couldn't understand one of the songs because of the strong Shrewsbury accent. To County, the chant sounded like 'I had a wheelbarrow…' and, struck by the bizarre nature of the lyrics, the visitors joined in. As the Notts supporters sang their new song, the team responded and came back to draw 2–2! As a result, the song earned cult status and is now the club's anthem on match-days.]

⚽ OLDHAM

If Robin Hood were real he'd be dead
If Robin Hood were real he'd be dead
If Robin Hood were real
Robin Hood were real
Robin Hood were real he'd be dead!

[Oldham taunt Nottingham Forest fans about the city's famous outlaw.]

⚽ PETERBOROUGH

Posh's surge up the Football League is down to a certain Mr Ferguson (Sir Alex's son, Darren) and exciting prospect George Boyd.

I saw my friend, the other day
He said he's seen the white Pele!
So I asked, 'Who is he?'
He goes by the name of George Boydie!
George Boydie! George Boydie! He goes by the name of George Boydie!

⚽ PLYMOUTH ARGYLE

Get a map, locate Plymouth, then laugh at this witty ditty to greet any travelling team to Home Park.

You dirty northern bastards!

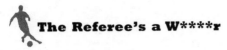

[Even the likes of Southampton and Brighton have been on the end of this one!]

⚽ PORT VALE

Robbie Williams may be a big Vale fan, but there have been no re-workings of 'Angels' yet. Instead, Elvis Presley's 'The Wonder of You' remains the classic chant at Vale Park. Arsenal have run out to this song since their move to the Emirates in 2006, but it remains very much a Vale anthem.

⚽ PORTSMOUTH

Sing 'Play up Pompey, Pompey play up' while wearing the Portsmouth blue and you'll fit in straight away. But if you really want to endear yourself to the south-coast masses, sing:

When Sol went up
To lift the FA Cup
I was there! I was there!

[In appreciation of Pompey's FA Cup-winning heroics in 2008.]

⚽ PRESTON NORTH END

Simple yet effective from the PNE die-hards here:

I am a Preston fan
I come from down Deepdale
And I can sing (what can you sing?)
I sing the PNE!!
Pi-a! Pi-a! PNE! PNE! PNE!

[To the tune of 'The Music Man' by Black Lace.]

⚽ QUEENS PARK RANGERS

Any song announcing your hatred for Chelsea or Fulham will go down well, but this simple Rs anthem gets Loftus Road rocking the most:

We are the Rangers boys! (clap, clap, clap, clap)
Stand up and make some noise!

⚽ READING

An old favourite in Berkshire remains the 'We wish you a happy season... we won't see you next year' take on the Christmas carol 'We Wish You a Merry Christmas', but following the emergence of English-born Turkey midfielder Jem Karacan, a Royals' version of Black Lace's 'Agadoo' has sprung up.

Karacan-can-can
He's our local kebab man
Karacan-can-can

The Referee's a W****r

He's our midfield ma-gi-cian
To the left
To the right
Try his doner meat tonight
He does halal of course
You should try his chilli sauce!

⚽ ROCHDALE

Rochdale celebrated their centenary season in 2007/08 and as they marched towards the League Two play-off final, expectation was high. Promotion would have been a perfect way to sign off 100 years of Rochdale FC, but Stockport ruined the party, beating Dale 3–2 in the final at Wembley. It was a similar story in the play-offs in the 2008/09 season as Gillingham beat them on their way to clinching promotion to League One. The Dale supporters can see the funny side, though, and have started something that – judging by their luck in the play-offs in recent years – could go on and on… and on… and, you get the message:

100 years… we fucked it up!
101… we fucked it up!
But for 102… we're going up!
For 102, we're going up!

⚽ ROTHERHAM

In a desperate bid to drum up some extra cash to save the ailing League Two side, the Millers enlisted the help of local band The Tivoli in 2008 to come up with a team song. In PR-speak, the anthem was part of a project to 'unite the club, local businesses and the Rotherham community with the aim of RUFC rising from the ashes of administration'. In layman's terms, the Millers wanted cash – fast. Even so, The Tivoli did a sterling job and their work is now heard regularly at the Don Valley Stadium in the form of terrace belter 'Drop Me Off in Rotherham'. The song is available to download online, if you so wish.

⚽ SCUNTHORPE UNITED

Scunny appointed former physio Nigel Adkins as permanent manager in December 2006, after a spell as caretaker boss following the departure of Brian Laws. Just four months later, he had won promotion to the Championship with three games to spare. United certainly took to Adkins and the following variation on Giuseppe Verdi's opera 'Rigoletto' is now a Glanford Park classic. See, this book is not just a vital piece of kit to take with you on match-days, it's also an important learning tool. Or something like that.

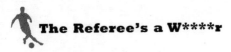

The Referee's a W****r

Who needs Mour-in-ho?
We've got our physio!
Who needs Mour-in-ho?
We've got our physio!

⚽ SHEFFIELD UNITED

You fill up my senses
Like a gallon of Magnet
Like a packet of Woodbines
Like a good pinch of snuff
Like a night out in Sheffield
Like a greasy chip butty
Like Sheffield United
Come fill me again
Na na na na na na, ooh!

[As we have seen, the Blades' memorable 'Greasy Chip Butty' song has been adopted by anyone from Accrington Stanley to Toronto FC. Its first known airing arrived in 1985 during an away match at Stoke City, where the Blades won 3–1. The song shouts out the virtues of the working-class north and all the delights that come with living in Sheffield. Magnet refers to John Smith's beer, while 'snuff' was seen as the working man's cocaine and was usually inhaled through the nose by steel workers. Blades' history expert John Garrett sums up the song thusly: 'Our Chinese sister club

Chengdu has their own version, but one thing is for sure – the whole of football know where they are and who they are playing. In the final line, we tell everyone about Sheffield. It is a football city and the birthplace of the modern game. Being a Blade brings its highs and lows, but the passion and commitment of following United is consuming.']

⚽ SHEFFIELD WEDNESDAY

When Carlos Tevez's goals for West Ham sent Sheffield United down in the 2007/08 season, the blue half of the Steel City had a new hero. 'There's only one Carlos Tevez' gets decent airtime, but Wednesdayites will do well to find something to dislodge their favourite anthem at Hillsborough:

And it's hi ho Sheffield Wednesday!

[To the tune of 'Hi Ho Silver Lining' by Jeff Beck.]

⚽ SHREWSBURY TOWN

The Welsh Bridge is a masonry arch viaduct in Shrewsbury that crosses the River Severn. So you can imagine Shrews' favourite song whenever Cardiff or Swansea are in town [which is not very often at the moment, although the song is still a favourite at New Meadow].

The Referee's a W****r

Always shit on the Welsh side of the bridge!

[To the tune of Monty Python's 'Always Look on the Bright Side of Life'.]

⚽ SOUTHAMPTON

Simple but effective…

Oh when the Saints (oh when the Saints)
Go marching in (go marching in)
Oh when the Saints go marching in
I want to be in that number!
Oh when the Saints go marching in!

⚽ SOUTHEND

Nice variation on 'The Animals Went in Two by Two' from the Shrimpers fans here:

When Southend United go out to play, sing up sing up
When Southend United go out to play, sing up sing up
When Southend United go out to play, we sing at home we sing away
We all follow the Essex boys in blue!

⚽ STOCKPORT COUNTY

We are everything in football
That people say is sad and wrong
But when we go to Edgeley Park
We'll sing our County song!
We'll raise our voice in chorus!
As we did in times before
And at Edgeley Park our greatest pride
Is the scarf my father wore!

Chorus:
It's forever being beautiful
And the colour's white and blue!
I wore it proudly round my neck
At Chesterfield and Crewe!
My father was a County fan
Like me grandfather before
And at Edgeley Park I love to wear
The scarf me father wore!

[chorus]

We will always follow County
To all games far and near!
And at Edgeley Park we'll sing those songs
That me father loved to hear!
We will raise our pints in memory
Of the games he loved to see

The Referee's a W****r

And at Edgeley Park, I'll wear the scarf
That me father left to me!

[chorus]

It's passed down the generations
Of my family!
Oh my granddad gave it to my dad
And me dad gave it to me
And when my time is over
And life's long race is run
I'll take the scarf from round my neck
And I'll pass it to my son!

[chorus]

🌑 STOKE CITY

The Potters fans were voted the loudest in the Premier League in their debut season as their anthem 'Delilah' blasted its way from the stands and out on to the pitch. It's no wonder only Manchester United, Chelsea, Everton and West Ham managed to come away from the Britannia Stadium with three points. There are many conflicting stories surrounding the birth of 'Delilah'. Legend has it that at an away game many moons ago, the travelling supporters were singing crude songs outside a pub before the match. Policemen pleaded with the fans to tone down their words and a lone voice duly obliged. She (apparently) sang 'Delilah', the fans caught on and the anthem was born. Other theories include the idea that the song developed when the Sensational Alex Harvey Band performed the song at Stoke's old ground, Victoria Park, in the 1970s and it caught on from there, while some Potters purists reckon a popular supporter called 'TJ' started singing it.

☉ SUNDERLAND

The Mackems have a bit of a reputation for being a yo-yo club in the Premier League (up one minute, down the next), which means the 'We're on our way' chant is never too far away from dominating the terraces. But one thing that will always remain constant is the affection the fans hold for former player and now chairman Niall Quinn. The love for big Niall is brilliantly summed up with:

Niall Quinn's disco pants are the best
They go up from his arse to his chest
They are better than Adam and the Ants
Niall Quinn's… disco pants!

[To the tune of the classic 'Here We Go'. If you don't know the tune to that – then why are you reading this book? Time for more history. The chant is not

one of those superbly random songs dreamed up on the spur of the moment (like Notts County's 'Wheelbarrow'), but a song born out of Quinn's decision to don a pair of cut-off jeans on a pre-season night out when he was playing for Manchester City in the 1990s. Blissfully unaware a group of City fans were watching him throw shapes on the dance floor of a club in Penola, Italy, Quinn danced the night away, complete with his 'disco pants'. And so the song was born. Quinn says: 'I was hardly aware I was being watched. The first performance of that song will follow me until the end of my career.']

⚽ SWANSEA CITY

They may play in the English Football League, but Swansea fans are always eager to add a little Welsh flavour to matches by singing a portion of the Welsh national anthem, 'Land of Our Fathers':

And we were singing
Hymns and chariots
Land of my fathers
AR HYD Y NOS! [All through the night]

⚽ SWINDON TOWN

See Lincoln's entry for Swindon's main favourite,

but the following take on 'Lord of the Dance' is just as popular at the County Ground.

Fight, fight wherever we may be
We are the boys from the West Country
We'll fight you all wherever we may be
Or we'll fight you all in the West Country!

⚽ TORQUAY

To any travelling fans to Plainmoor who couldn't tell their bucket and spade from their elbow [and to the tune of 'Guantanamera']:

Have you ever seen a beach!

⚽ TOTTENHAM HOTSPUR

Backed by a traditionally strong Jewish following, the Spurs fans constantly declare their love for the 'Yid' army. 'Yid' is a slang term to denote followers of Judaism, but far from being offended by it, Tottenham fans pride themselves on using it. Following a 4–4 draw away at bitter rivals Arsenal in 2008, the Spurs fans dreamt up a new chant almost immediately after Aaron Lennon's 93rd-minute equaliser. Tottenham were losing 3–1 and 4–2, but came back from the dead to claim a memorable point.

 **The Referee's a W****r**

Chim chiminey
Chim chiminey
Chim chim cheroo!
Bentley from forty and Lennon from two!

The draw clearly had an effect at Spurs – not only did it yield a new terrace favourite, but the club also produced DVDs commemorating the fact they had claimed a point at the Emirates.

⚽ TRANMERE

If you want to come out of Prenton Park alive, don't for one minute suggest Tranmere fans may be Scousers...

Build a bonfire, build a bonfire!
Put the Scousers on the top
Put Benitez in the middle
And we'll burn the fucking lot!

⚽ WALSALL

She wore, she wore, she wore a yellow ribbon
She wore it from the spring time
Till the merry month of May
And when I asked her why the hell she wore it
She wore it for the Walsall fan, far, far away
Far away, far away, when the Walsall boys play away

220

Doing The 92

We won't be far away, far away, far away!

⚽ WATFORD

The Hornets regard Graham Taylor as an almost God-like being – and with good reason. He once took Watford from the old Fourth Division to the First in only five years and also masterminded their foray into the UEFA Cup in the 1980s. In his second spell at the club, he took Watford to the Premier League. He's now a director at Vicarage Road and his achievements at the club have never gone unnoticed.

There was a town where I was born
That had a yellow super team
They had a man called Graham Taylor
That took us to the Premier League
We all support a yellow super team, a yellow super team, a yellow super team!
We all support a yellow super team, a yellow super team, a yellow super team!

[To the tune of 'Yellow Submarine' by The Beatles.]

⚽ WEST BROM

Think of West Brom and you think of 'Boing, Boing Baggies' as well as the predictable Aston Villa

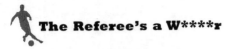

hatred, expertly summed up with this ode to rookie striker Ishmael Miller:

Is this the way to hammer Villa?
With lots of goals from Ishmael Miller!
We'll be shitting on Aston Villa
When Ishmael Miller scores for us!

[To the tune of 'Is This The Way to Amarillo' by Tony Christie.]

⚽ WEST HAM

Rumours Michael Jackson wanted this song at his funeral are, to date, completely unfounded:

I'm forever blowing bubbles
Pretty bubbles in the air
They fly so high
They reach the sky
Then like my dreams
They fade and die
Fortune's always hiding
I've looked everywhere
I'm forever blowing bubbles
Pretty bubbles in the air
UNITED! UNITED! UNITED!

⚽ WIGAN

In the 2007/08 and 2008/09 seasons, Wigan finished bottom in the league for average attendance. It's no secret the Lancashire town prefers rugby to the beautiful game, which is summed up well by this amusing line of self-deprecation from the Latics fans:

Shall we score a try for you!

⚽ WOLVES

There are numerous tributes to Wolves legend Steve Bull at Molineux but 'Those Were the Days' remains the anthem of choice in the Black Country. Originally sung by Mary Hopkins, Wolves fans change the final line to:

For we're the Wolves, oh yes we are the Wolves!

⚽ WYCOMBE WANDERERS

John Mousinho has become a firm fans' favourite since his arrival from Brentford in June 2008 and the Wycombe faithful earn points for this simple but effective variation on Giuseppe Verdi's opera 'Rigoletto'.

Who needs Mou-rin-ho? We've got Mou-sin-ho!

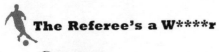

The Referee's a W****r

☉ YEOVIL

The Glovers have grown accustomed to singing 'We are staying up, I say we are staying up' in the past few seasons (in 2007/08 they avoided relegation from League One by two points, a year later it was four), but when they're not voicing their optimism for the future, they rip off Arsenal's 'Ooh to be a Gooner' anthem.

Ooh to
Ooh to be
Ooh to be a
Glover!

Phew! That was hard work. But don't get too comfy, up next is some pretty X-rated stuff…

CHAPTER FIVE:
X-RATED

⚽ THE REFEREE'S A WANKER

A football match would not be complete without shouting at the referee. If you've missed out on promotion or a place in the next round, it's far easier to slate the man in black other than the real villains: your actual team.

Refs may have harshly sent off your centre-back, disallowed a crucial goal or failed to give that penalty – or perhaps just turning up is enough to enrage some fans.

Retired ref Jeff Winter released an autobiography with the tongue-in-cheek title *Who's The Bastard in the Black?*, which sums up the attitude we often have towards officials. But fans are not alone in their dislike of the man in the middle. Speaking to ref Jeff, Sir Alex Ferguson once said:

The Referee's a W****r

'Back to your usual self, Jeff, fucking useless!'

While Ferguson's former captain Steve Bruce had his own views on Winter:

'He drives me nuts. An absolute prat – and you can print that as well.'

With such hatred spilling from the mouths of managers, it's no wonder we follow suit. The insults can range from the petty 'you need glasses' to morale-crushing tirades – just ask Graham Poll.

⚽ WORLD CUP 2006

Poll was at the pinnacle of his career in Germany in the summer of 2006. He had officiated in the previous World Cup, in Japan and South Korea, and had also refereed at Euro 2000. After an impressive couple of performances, he was widely regarded to be in with a great chance of taking charge of the final. All he had to do was make sure everything went smoothly in a group match between Croatia and Australia. Then Josep Simunic came along.

Ref Poll, dubbed 'The Thing from Tring', showed the Croatia midfielder a yellow card – three times. Having already sent off three players and incorrectly allowing a goal for Australia (Harry Kewell was clearly offside), he dropped the mother of all

clangers and failed to send Simunic off after giving him a second warning.

He eventually did send the defender off, for a third cautionable offence, after the final whistle. Poll was sent home from the World Cup and never refereed at an international tournament again. He apparently couldn't sleep following the nightmare performance and when he did return to the game, crowds in the Premier League revelled in the chance to remind him of his blunder:

World Cup... and you fucked it up!

[To the tune of 'Guantanamera'.]

Graham Poll is an arsehole!
Graham Poll is an arsehole!
He comes from Tring
Doesn't know a thing!
Walking in a wanker wonderland!

[To the tune of 'Winter Wonderland'.]

⚽ BEST OF THE REST

These classic chants would also probably sum up fans' feelings towards Poll following his cataclysmic card cock-up:

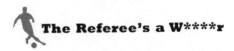

The Referee's a W****r

You don't know what you're doing!

Who's the bastard in the black?

The referee's a wanker!

Are you [team] in disguise?

⚽ DON'T CRAMP CLATTENBURG'S STYLE

Official Mark Clattenburg suffered cramp during a match between Arsenal and Liverpool in 2006 and upon hearing this chant from the Gunners fans, he managed to crack a smile:

You're not fit to referee!

⚽ X-RATED

In May 2009, a man and a 14-year-boy were among those found guilty of homophobic abuse directed towards Portsmouth defender Sol Campbell during a match between Portsmouth and Tottenham the previous September. Both were banned from attending matches for three years and had to pay costs of £400.

To say Spurs fans hate Sol is a little like saying World War II was a bit of a skirmish. The supporters often sing vile songs about him, with racist,

homophobic and threatening lyrics. The reason for their fury? The defender left White Hart Lane for Arsenal in 2000. Campbell was labelled a 'Judas' for moving to Spurs' bitter London rivals. Any player who moves between rival teams will invariably run the gauntlet of hate when he returns to play against his former club – vitriol is the price you pay for turning your back on the fans. But Campbell's treatment really has been awful.

Spurs repeatedly sing about wanting to see Campbell hanging from a tree, and lace their hate-filled chants with cries of 'Judas c**t'. Standing near the away end at Fratton Park when Spurs were in town in September 2008, you could see the Spurs fans' faces contorted with rage whenever Campbell touched the ball. They even chanted that they wouldn't care if he contracted HIV.

The songs and chants are barbaric, but they should be taken with a big pinch of salt. Just because the Spurs followers sing about how much they would like to kill Campbell, it doesn't mean their threats will be carried out. These men (and women, it must be said) have ordinary lives, jobs and friends. Football gives them the chance to escape their mundane existence and live the dream for 90 minutes every weekend. Everyday life is banished amid a chorus of booing, screaming, chanting and scheming.

Once you take your seat in the Stretford End, the

Kop, the Rainham End or the Arthur Wait stand, you are no longer 'Dad', 'Paul from HR' or 'Sharron the wholesaler', you're a 'Yiddo', part of the 'Republik of Mancunia', a 'Kopite' or a member of Gillingham's 'Pikey Army'. You're a football fan. Social etiquette flies out the window. 'Paul from HR' wouldn't label Sol Campbell a 'Judas c**t' if he moved departments in the workplace but, thrust into a football stadium, Paul becomes someone else – a fan – and with it comes agony, ecstasy and jealousy.

Distasteful chants aren't pretty, but they're just part of the football experience. Where's the fun in Everton fans saying, 'Oh, that Torres chap, I think he is a talented fellow'? They are more likely to claim the Spaniard 'wears a frock and loves the cock' because he plays for Liverpool, Everton's sworn enemies. Berating the players is part of the fun. Unfortunately, some unsavoury songs – when banter spills over into the obscene – have blurred the distinction between what is and what is not acceptable.

Fans are like tribes, with a determination to nail their colours to the mast, and chants act as a way of announcing your allegiance to the team – a type of battlecry. They are not intended to mimic reality; far from it. Everton sing about their wish to 'hang the Kopites one by one … On the banks of the Royal Blue Mersey', but, of course, not one Liverpool fan has ever actually been hanged by the Mersey river

since this song first gained notoriety in the 1960s.

While the song from Everton outlines hatred – geographically inspired – of Liverpool, there are instances when fans across the country put their rivalries aside and join in for choruses. And in the case of Eduardo, the result is not particularly pleasant. In February 2008, Arsenal's faltering title challenge suffered a mortal blow when they drew 2–2 away at Birmingham. William Gallas reacted to the draw with the mother of all hissy-fits as he sat in the centre circle at the sound of the full-time whistle, fighting back the tears.

But the game will be remembered for one thing and one thing only – Eduardo. The Arsenal striker was scythed down by Martin Taylor, the tackle so horrendous it left the Brazilian-born Croatian with a shattered leg. There were fears he would never walk again, let alone play, as Eduardo suffered a horrific double leg-break. The sight of Eduardo's ankle hanging by a thread was shocking, as was the lack of compassion from anti-Arsenal fans, who greeted the news with chants of: 'Eduardo, whoa! Eduardo, whoa! He used to have silky skills, now he walks like Heather Mills.' Other chants included a variation on the hit song 'Monster' by The Automatic, with the lyrics: 'What's that coming out of your sock? Is it your ankle, is it your ankle?'

Thankfully, not only did Eduardo manage to walk again, he also scored in his comeback match against

Cardiff in the FA Cup in 2009. Yes, the chants are insensitive, but who's to say they didn't inspire the striker to come back and ram the tasteless words right back down the opposition fans' throats?

Gareth Southgate, the Middlesbrough manager, reckons the debate about tasteless chants is a double-edged sword. During a Tyne-Tees derby in the 2008/09 season, Middlesbrough striker Mido suffered chants of 'Mido, Mido, he's got a bomb you know' from Newcastle supporters. This wasn't because the Egyptian was a Muslim, but because he was a player the Newcastle fans feared. He was the best Middlesbrough had to offer in terms of an attacking threat, hence the Toon's dislike. Southgate said at the time: 'When something like that happens, I am sure the player thinks "I'll show you".'

Manchester City star Shaun Wright-Phillips put Southgate's words into practice in March 2009 following an almighty onslaught from Aston Villa supporters during a match at Villa Park. England star Wright-Phillips is the adopted son of Arsenal legend Ian Wright but, despite being a more than able performer for his country and a tireless charity fundraiser, the Villa fans are more interested in enquiring about the winger's family life. To the tune of 'Where's Your Mama Gone' the Villains fans sung 'Who's your real dad? Who's your real dad?' It is not beyond the realms of possibility that one of the Villa

fans that day had, or knew someone who had an adoptive father, but in the pressure-cooker that is Premier League football, such details were obviously forgotten. At least SWP made the haters eat their words when he netted City's second goal in a 2–0 victory.

The personal lives of footballers provide supporters with some fearsome ammunition when it comes to castigating them from the stands. If a player has been pictured in the papers following a boozy night out, he can expect a pasting the next time he emerges on to the field. Sometimes, however, the antics – or alleged antics – of players can be seized upon by supporters who have a flagrant disregard for the facts.

A case in point would be Arsenal ace Robin van Persie, who spent time in a Dutch prison in 2005 amid allegations that he sexually assaulted a woman. The charges were dropped and there is no evidence or suggestion that he was involved in any assault of any kind. Not that it mattered to thousands of fans up and down the country, who goaded the Dutch striker with: 'Van Persie, when the girl says no – molest her!' (To the tune of 'Rewind' by the Artful Dodger and Craig David).

Another instance of fans shunning the facts in favour of a cutting put-down arrived in 2004 when Leicester City were playing in the Premier League. Three Leicester players – Paul Dickov, Keith

Gillespie and Frank Sinclair – were accused of serious sexual misconduct while on a pre-season bonding trip to Spain. The charges were subsequently dropped, but try telling that to anyone travelling to Leicester during the 2004/05 season, who used that age-old favourite 'Guantanamera' as the tune for: 'Score in La Manga! You couldn't score in La Manga!'

There can be no arguing, however, about the facts behind one song aimed at Graham Rix. In 1999, Chelsea coach Rix was sent to prison for 12 months for having unlawful sex with a 15-year-old girl. He served six months before going back to his job at Stamford Bridge. Rix suffered a barrage of abuse from the stands and, to the tune of 'If You Tolerate This' by the Manic Street Preachers, this chant followed him everywhere until he left England for Spain: 'If you tolerate Rix/Then your children will be next!'

It's pretty hard-hitting stuff and, while the parents of the girl in question wouldn't find the song remotely funny, it raised a smile or two up and down the country, particularly when the shamed Rix seemed to squirm in the dugout as the chants grew louder. As we have seen, any indiscretion will get flagged up by supporters, who have the right to voice their views. Freedom of speech and all that.

However, there's a difference between freedom of speech and tasteless abuse. One of the very cornerstones of British democracy is our ability to

vent our frustration and say what we like, but when there's a fierce local rivalry between teams, chants can take a twisted turn for the worst.

Take Moscow 2008, for example. John Terry stood on the cusp of history. He had the Champions League firmly in his grasp but, instead of smashing the ball past Manchester United goalkeeper Edwin van der Sar and winning the Cup, he slipped and booted Chelsea's hopes of glory away. The Chelsea captain, who is usually portrayed as being 'brave as a lion, Mr Chelsea', did nothing for his street cred when he blubbed all over Moscow, looking like a little boy who'd lost his mum in the supermarket.

Seeing 'Mr Chelsea' cry was enough for most supporters, but Fulham supporters took Terry-baiting to the next level with this below-the-belt chant: 'John Terry's a wanker/He is a fucking prick/And when he went to Moscow, he missed the winning kick/He couldn't hit the target, he fell on to his bum/To leave their hopes of victory/As dead as Lampard's mum.'

Lampard lost mother Patricia to pneumonia in 2008 and quite why the Fulham supporters had to bring her into their dislike for Terry is anyone's guess. It rhymes, obviously, but that's a tenuous link to a song that has done the rounds at Craven Cottage. Admittedly, in mitigation, a string of Cottagers fans have blasted the use of the song on the club's internet messageboard.

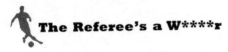

Next up in the long list of shame is the ditty used to antagonise Arsenal manager Arsène Wenger. Wenger has a reputation for putting his faith in the youth team and giving his 'kids' a chance to shine. They're not actually children, they are all above 16, but the football lexicon demands that people refer to them as kids, and Wenger's youth policy has inspired the following chant, which Manchester United fans have been singing since 1999: 'There's only one Arsène Wenger! One Arsène Wenger! With a packet of sweets and a cheeky smile/Wenger is a fucking paedophile!' (Sung to the tune of 'Winter Wonderland'). Wenger has long voiced his extreme displeasure at the song, and you can't blame him given the fact that he has never had anything remotely to do with paedophilia.

On one hand, the chants can be described as humorous, designed to wind up the opposition and raise a giggle, but it's easy to understand why some people want hefty fines or even suspensions handed down to clubs whose fans get out of hand, when you hear some of the more unsavoury offerings from supporters. Witness the racist: 'Ooh Adebayor/Ooh Adebayor!/Your dad washes elephants/Your mum is a whore.'

Adebayor had to endure that disgraceful chant when he lined up for Manchester City against former club Arsenal in September 2009. The Togo star had enraged Arsenal fans with his move to

Eastlands because, in their eyes, he had gone for the money after what can only be described as a substandard career at the Emirates.

City's 4–2 win over Arsenal was eventful to say the least. Apart from the nouveau-riche club announcing themselves to be a genuine force in the league, the game will always be remembered for Adebayor's outrageous raking of Robin van Persie's face and THAT celebration. The furore that erupted from the Arsenal fans following Adebayor's decision to run the length of the pitch to celebrate his City goal in front of them was unbelievable.

Adebayor was portrayed as the anti-Christ for inciting the Arsenal fans, but the travelling supporters had been singing racist songs about his family throughout the match. The player rightly suggested that if someone had been subjected to such abuse in the street, they would probably have a go back. The old adage 'Don't dish it out if you can't take it' never seemed more apt.

When a couple of Leeds fans were stabbed to death during a trip to Galatasaray in 2000 it was a tragic instance of when football rivalry spills over into the barbaric. And things didn't improve back at home. Incensed at the Leeds fans' long-running mockery of the Munich and Hillsborough disasters, Manchester United and Liverpool fans joined forces – for once – and warned the Elland Road masses about future trips to Turkey: 'Always look

out for Turks carrying knives! Do-do, do-do, do-do-do-be-do!'

The song, to the tune of 'Always Look on the Bright Side of Life' from *The Life of Brian*, is a typical response from United and Liverpool fans, who have been subjected to abuse from many clubs' supporters in the past. 'Always look on the runway for ice' is the Leeds anthem of choice when referring to the tragic Munich air disaster in 1958, which claimed the lives of 23 people, including eight Manchester United players. Duncan Edwards, who would have surely gone on to be mentioned in the same breath as Pele or Diego Maradona, sadly died from his injuries 15 days after the crash, but moronic supporters don't really care about the fact that Edwards would have probably helped England to win more than the one World Cup they currently have to their name. He was a Manchester United player – a cardinal sin in the minds of anyone who doesn't support the club.

Manchester United are one of the most successful – and hated – clubs in world football. Perhaps the hatred has something to do with their successful, yet abrasive, manager Sir Alex Ferguson, or the glut of silverware in the Old Trafford trophy cabinet, or the fact that a significant amount of their supporters do not herald from Manchester. From Surrey to Singapore, United have a following most teams could only dream of.

The almost universal dislike for United is represented in a variety of ways and, while most of it can be put down to jealousy and tongue-in-cheek humour, there is simply no excusing the way in which some supporters refer to the club and their fans as 'Munichs'. The air disaster in 1958 did not just claim the lives of Manchester United players and staff. Manchester City fans' chant of 'Carlos Tevez is a Blue, he hates Munichs' is not only vile but hypocritical and factually wrong – the Argentine striker has gone on record numerous times saying he loves United and their fans.

Tevez, like Sol Campbell, crossed the divide and moved from one part of the city to another when he moved from United to City in the summer of 2009. Towards the end of the 2008/09 campaign, Old Trafford regularly reverberated with chants of 'Fergie, Fergie sign him up' as the calls for Ferguson to sign Tevez on a permanent deal grew louder by the day.

But Fergie didn't sign him up, allowing Tevez to become the new hero at City and in his debut for the club, the Blue half of Manchester laughed as City fans ironically sang the chant that the Red half had made their own. 'Fergie, Fergie sign him up' echoed around the City of Manchester Stadium as Tevez entered the pitch.

But the 'Munichs' chant wrecked what would have been a light-hearted dig at City's rivals. Indeed,

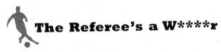

The Referee's a W****r

Frank Swift, the former Manchester City goalkeeper, died in the Munich air crash, making the fans' chant sound even more ridiculous.

In 2000, City's official match-day programme referred to United supporters as 'Munichs' and, amid the outrage that followed, City's chairman at the time, David Bernstein, said: 'It was a mistake and we are sorry for any offence caused. Among other things, we will never forget that Frank Swift was killed in the disaster.'

But Manchester United supporters shouldn't think they can take the moral high ground – United fans have also been guilty of ruining the match-day experience for respectable supporters by chanting about the tragic Hillsborough disaster, which claimed the lives of 96 innocent football fans in 1989. A small minority of United (and Leeds) fans have sung 'It's just... a little crush' to the tune of Jennifer Paige's hit song.

United fans also sing 'Without killing anybody, we've won it three times', which refers to the number of European Cups the club have won and is also a dig at the Heysel disaster, in which 39 innocent fans (mostly Juventus) died before the European Cup final between Liverpool and Juve in 1985.

As a result of the tragedy, English clubs were placed under an indefinite ban from all European competitions by UEFA, while Liverpool were

excluded for an additional year, with some of their fans prosecuted for manslaughter.

Elsewhere, Arsenal supporters (among others) are quick to proclaim they still possess their foreskins whenever Tottenham come to town. There is a strong Jewish following among Spurs fans, who have grown accustomed to hearing: 'We'll be running round Tottenham with our willies hanging out/Singing 'I've got a foreskin haven't you? (Fucking Jew)'.

No wonder Millwall fans sing 'No one likes us' – their choice of chants leaves a lot to be desired. The south Londoners have been known to like a scrap or two and when the police come to cool things down, Millwall diehards try to wind them up with a vicious adaptation of 'London Bridge is Falling Down': 'Harry Roberts is our friend, is our friend, is our friend/ Harry Roberts is our friend, he kills coppers'. Roberts was the instigator of the 'Massacre of Braybrook Street', a triple murder of policemen in 1966.

Excusing these chants as a symbol of an entrenched rivalry is a feeble attempt to mask these vile terrace taunts, but there is no social etiquette when it comes to following a football team. Once you've passed through the turnstiles and taken your seat, you are free to sing whatever you want and while the masses will delight us with fantastic tributes to their star players, the minority will abuse their right to free speech.

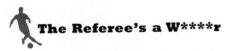

But let's not let the ill-advised songs detract from the real humour and intelligence of finely crafted pieces of terrace wisdom. Football fans are not part of the PC brigade, which makes the culture of the football chant all the more amusing. The beautiful game gives us the opportunity of escapism, which means the odd rude word here and stupid song there is commonplace.

CHAPTER SIX:
EXTRA TIME

Your lungs are red raw from all the shouting, singing and referee-baiting and your creative juices have flowed for the whole 90 minutes, dreaming of new ditties and cruel put-downs.

So what's next? Well, if you've done the 92, hailed halibut, sung about tampons and become sick of 'Guantanamera', this section is for you. Footie fans are not the only ones capable of raising a chuckle or two – anyone from the players themselves to stadium announcers and football commentators have provided us with valuable snips of comedy gold.

Don't leave your seat early, there's still time for some more action – and kicking 'Extra Time' off in style is England striker Peter Crouch:

Interviewer: Peter, what would you have been if you

failed to make it as a footballer?
Peter Crouch: A virgin.

And now, Wayne Rooney – what would you have done had it all gone wrong as a footballer?

'I haven't a clue what else I would have done. I wasn't really the best in school. I always enjoyed RE, so maybe a priest.'

Crouch and Rooney almost steal the comedy crown away from David Beckham, but Becks just manages to keep on top with this stunning salvo of stupidity:

Interviewer: David, who would you say are the main influences on your career?
David Beckham: My parents – they've been there for me ever since I was seven.

Interviewer: What plans have you got for your baby?
David Beckham: We're definitely going to get him christened, but I'm not sure into what religion yet.

Yes. He really did say that.

Beckham's heir-apparent in the England set-up used to be David Bentley, but then we realised he wasn't that good, or committed enough, to play for the Three Lions. He declined to go to the Euro 2007

Under-21 tournament because he was 'too tired'. However, at least Bents can rival Becks when it comes to dropping howlers in interviews:

'I don't want to be playing in the Under-21s forever.'

[Bentley, clearly without a grasp of the ageing process, in an interview before Blackburn's FA Cup fifth-round replay against Arsenal in 2007.)

James Milner, on the other hand, loves playing for the young Three Lions side. He has amassed 46 Under-21 caps – an England record – but he's clearly not picked for his intelligence:

'I would give my right arm to pull on the England shirt.'

Now that would be one hell of a struggle.

⚽ SIR BOBBY ROBSON 1933-2009

Sir Bobby proved that nice guys can finish first. Football lost a true gentleman in July 2009 when the former England manager lost his fight against cancer at the fifth time of asking. Bobby won the FA Cup and UEFA Cup with Ipswich, took England to within one kick of reaching the World Cup final in 1990 and led his beloved Newcastle to the Champions League.

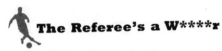

Everyone was richer for knowing him. A true hero and leader – a man capable of raising spirits simply by walking into the room. His legacy lives on with the Sir Bobby Robson Foundation, which raises money for the early detection of cancer.

And we will always remember him for his cracking quotes and all the hilarious tales from his distinguished career as a manager. Topping the list is this story from Shola Ameobi, whom Robson managed while he was at Newcastle:

Interviewer: Shola, do you have any nicknames?
Shola Ameobi: No.
Interviewer: So what do your Newcastle team-mates call you?
Shola Ameobi: They just call me Shola.
Interviewer: What about Sir Bobby Robson? What does he call you?
Shola Ameobi: Carl Cort!

⚽ BOBBY'S GEMS

'The first 90 minutes of a football match are the most important.'

'Well, we scored nine goals – you can't score more than that.'

'The margin is very marginal.'

'If you count your chickens before they've hatched, they won't lay an egg.'

'We didn't underestimate them, they were just a lot better than we thought.'

'Tottenham have impressed me: they haven't thrown in the towel even though they have been under the gun.'

'I would have given my right arm to be a pianist.'

'Gary Speed has never played better, never looked fitter, never been older.'

'Ray Wilkins' day will come one night.'

⚽ SIR BOBBY ON HIS KNIGHTHOOD

Alan Brazil: 'I'm delighted to say we've got Sir Bobby Robson on the end of the phone, fresh from getting his knighthood at Buckingham Palace. Bobby – terrific news.'
Sir Bobby Robson: 'What is?'
Brazil: 'You know, getting the old sword on the shoulder from Prince Charlie.'
Sir Bobby: Eh? [Long pause] 'Oh yeah… well, it was a day I'll never forget.'

⚽ AND FINALLY, THE LAST WORD

'Maybe not goodbye… but farewell.'

⚽ I DON'T WANT TO INSULT SUNDERLAND…

But Bordeaux president Jean-Louis Triaud would love to. Speaking about rumours linking striker Marouane Chamakh with a move to Wearside, he said:

'What the fuck would he do at Sunderland? You have heard him say he will only sign for a big English club. I don't want to insult Sunderland, but I don't even know where they finished last season.'

⚽ A VERY, VERY UNPLEASANT IMAGE…

Wigan manager Steve Bruce, after his side were beaten 3–0 by Arsenal in 2008:

'They've kicked our backsides; we've got to lick our wounds.'

⚽ TOP OF THE CLASS…?

Frank Lampard has 12 GCSEs at grade C or above, including an A* in Latin. Strange, considering his comments about Didier Drogba's coin-throwing

against Burnley in 2008:

'There's two sides to it.'

⚽ WORD FROM A SHRINKING VIOLET...

Manchester City's much-publicised pursuit of Chelsea's John Terry in the summer of 2009 grabbed a hatful of headlines, but nothing can top this from Oasis frontman and City fan Liam Gallagher:

'I don't like John Terry and I never have. He's got funny eyes and he's a cry baby. He's also a Cockney.'

⚽ WHO SAID AMERICANS KNOW NOTHING ABOUT 'SOCCER'?

Following a US Open Cup... yes, *cup*, victory over Rochester Rhinos in 2009, DC United's Jaime Moreno gave reporters a well-crafted insight into the victory:

'Obviously we are delighted to get the three points.'

⚽ WHEN A MAN LOVES A WOMAN...

Kolo Toure does his best Percy Sledge impression upon signing for Manchester City from Arsenal:

'When you love a woman and she gives you back the love you are really happy and that's what I can see at City. They have given me the love and I'm really delighted to bring them back the love.'

⚽ FOR YOUR LICENCE FEE...

Where shall we start?

'Justice is a dish best served cold.'

[Garth Crooks on BBC's *Score*. I think the word you're looking for is 'dunce', I mean, 'revenge', Garth...]

'They've got a teletepathic, teletelpathic, pathetic, well it's not pathetic... oh just forget it...'

[Graham Taylor on BBC 5Live, failing miserably to describe the telepathic understanding of Barcelona duo Xavi and Andres Iniesta.]

'It was that game that put the Everton ship back on the road.'

[BBC 5Live commentator Alan Green gets ludicrously mixed up in his attempt to describe Everton's 3–2 defeat to Aston Villa in 2008. David Moyes' boys reacted well despite the defeat, leading to Green's silly assertion.]

'Brazil are so good they are running around the pitch, playing with themselves.'

[An oldie, but a goodie from John Motson.]

'Soder's lost his fizz, hasn't he?'

[Excellent work from Chris Waddle, commentating on England U-21's Euro 2009 semi-final against Sweden.]

'Forget Huckleberry Finn, Moby Dick, Last of the Mohicans, Mickey Mouse and Sleeping Beauty...'

[BBC3 commentator Steve Wilson gets a little carried away as he tries to put USA's remarkable 2009 Confederations Cup run into perspective.]

'One of the world's best defenders trying to play offside there... oh no, it's Dossena...'

[Heard during the half-time analysis of Brazil's 2009 Confederations Cup clash with Italy. Lee Dixon brilliantly backtracks after finding out the player in question was Liverpool flop Andrea Dossena.]

'Kitson's pass was that good Sidwell didn't even have to move for it, he just ran straight to it...'

[Dixon again, describing Steve Sidwell's one-two

with Dave Kitson on *Match of the Day 2*. Did he move? Did he have to run? What did he do?]

'These Italian players will be a year older in a year's time.'

[Dixon's pal on the BBC sofa, Martin Keown.]

'Casper Ankergren's a bit of a Dracula-type keeper... doesn't like crosses'

[Andy Ritchie excels while commentating on Leeds v Hartlepool for BBC Radio Leeds.]

'If [Arsène] Wenger is still here in ten years and Arsenal haven't won any trophies, will he still be here?'

[Steve Claridge on BBC 5Live.]

'Arsenal's first touch and movement is amazing. I hope the people listening are watching this.'

[Chris Waddle, speaking on the *radio*, during the Bolton v Arsenal FA Cup tie in 2007.]

⚽ YOUR LICENCE FEE (AGAIN) AND PRIORITIES

It's Liverpool v Arsenal, April 2009. It's tight, tense and three goals apiece. Anything other than a win for Liverpool would surely mean another league title for Manchester United.

Arsenal are having a real go, inspired by the quite brilliant Andrey Arshavin, who has already scored a hat-trick.

BBC Radio 5Live listeners are gagging for expert analysis, desperate to know where this match may be going.

Alan Green: Mark, it's 3–3. Who'd you fancy?
Mark Lawrenson: Britney!

[The match ended 4–4.]

⚽ MARK LAWRENSON AND ARGUING

'There's no argument, arguably he's in the form of his life.'

[Discussing Nicolas Anelka's form for Chelsea during the 2008/09 season.]

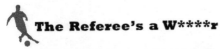

⚽ FROM THE DEPARTMENT OF THE BLEEDIN' OBVIOUS...

David Pleat, commentating on BBC Radio 5Live, in the match between Tottenham and Manchester United in September 2009:

'Home sides tend to be very supportive of their favourite team.'

⚽ AND FINALLY...

'This is a real cat and carrot situation'

[Pleat, again. Me neither...]

⚽ QUALITY INSIGHT FROM SETANTA

No wonder they went bust...

'Not many teams can bring on Rooney and Ronaldo when they're 2-0 up...'

[Could *any* team other than Manchester United have done this, Jon Champion?]

⚽ WHAT TO EXPECT FROM SETANTA'S SUCCESSORS

From the 2009/10 season, Disney-owned ESPN televised live Premier League matches and they got lucky with their first match of the season – Arsenal's 6–1 hammering of Everton. Perhaps it's good fortune they had action on the field to talk about, considering this obscure comment from Paul Masefield on ESPN's *Football Focus* programme, referring to Rafael Benitez's style of management at Liverpool:

'He's got to put his foot down with an iron fist.'

⚽ WHAT WE WANT MORE OF FROM SETANTA'S SUCCESSORS

'Bendtner proves how useless he is by collecting a Fabregas ball on the edge of the box before turning and passing to Rooney...'

[ESPN.com show everyone how to be impartial in their 'Gamecast' coverage of Manchester United v Arsenal in the 2009 Champions League semi-final.]

⚽ SPEAKING OF IMPARTIALITY

Courtesy of Portsmouth radio station Quay 107.4,

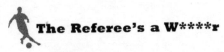
covering Portsmouth's clash with Manchester United in 2007:

'Cristiano Ronaldo, no doubt a fantastic player, but look at him sitting down in the box, looking like he's going to cry... like a little girl. No doubting his talent, but he is a squinny [a whiner]. An absolute squinny...'

⚽ BAD...

Theo Walcott's inclusion in the England squad for 2006 World Cup raised many eyebrows. The youngster, then 17, had never played for Arsenal and Sven-Göran Eriksson admitted he had not seen Walcott play before picking him. His call-up was big news and *Daily Mirror* tipster Derek McGovern covered the story in the following manner:

'It's an incredible rise to stardom. At 17, you're more likely to get a call from Michael Jackson than Sven-Göran Eriksson.'

⚽ GOD-AWFUL GLENN

Faith-healing advocate Glenn Hoddle has a reputation for putting his foot in it. Remember his unfortunate comments regarding the disabled? Let's refresh your memory:

'You and I have been physically given two hands and two legs and half-decent brains. Some people have not been born like that for a reason. The karma is working from another lifetime. I have nothing to hide about that. It is not only people with disabilities. What you sow, you have to reap.'

Glenn's stupidity got the better of him again when he was invited on to TalkSPORT radio to discuss the holy trinity of Samuel Eto'o, Thierry Henry and Lionel Messi, ahead of the Champions League final against Manchester United. The trio had shared over 90 goals between them that season, leading Hoddle to say:

'I'm surprised, but that's not surprising.'

⚽ MORE FROM TALKSPORT

Brazilian striker Jo banged in five goals during his loan spell at Everton in the 2008/09 season and TalkSPORT presenter Mike Parry was impressed with him. If only he could have thought a little harder before he started praising the new Toffees hero:

'Jo has become a national hero, on one half of Merseyside.'

The Referee's a W****r

⚽ UNBELIEVABLE, JEFF

Soccer Saturday wouldn't be the same without Chris 'Unbelievable, Jeff' Kamara. The half-decent player turned hilariously inept pundit is capable of making the most exciting match thoroughly incomprehensible for the viewers.

Kammy's most memorable efforts:

'Tense and nervous aren't the words, Jeff, but they are, if you know what I mean...'

[During the first half of the Sunderland v Hull game.]

'You've got to hand it to West Brom, Jeff. They're defending like, like – well, urm...like beavers, really...'

[Kamara and his dam sayings...]

'He had it on a plate, he had the sausage, bacon and eggs on it as well, but he couldn't take it...'

[Not content with using the clichéd line 'he had it on a plate' to describe a gilt-edged opportunity, Kammy goes off on one as he tries to describe a missed chance during Portsmouth's clash with Fulham in 2006.]

'This match is real end-to-end stuff, Jeff. But, unfortunately for Forest, it's all up their end.'

[There's no end of confusion as Kammy tries to describe the action involving Nottingham Forest.]

⚽ 'ADE-CASH-WHORE'

Emmanuel Adebayor infuriated Arsenal fans with his constant flirtations with AC Milan in the summer of 2008. He stayed for one more year before missing out on his dream move to Italy – he moved to Manchester City instead. Speaking about his temptation to join Milan, the Togo striker said:

'For me that must be something special. It is like a boy being told Beyonce is looking for them.'

[So what does that make City then? Amy Winehouse?]

⚽ PAUL SCHOLES

Put Scholes in the Manchester United midfield and he's like a man possessed, spraying passes left, right and centre. Put him in front of a camera, however, and Scholesy looks like someone who's won the lottery and forgotten to tick the 'no publicity' box.

Clive Tyldesley is probably glad Scholes shuns the media spotlight. If he didn't, the midfield star would

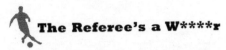

undoubtedly have a few things to say to the ITV commentator, who once said:

'It looks like Scholes is walking a bit gingerly...'

[From an Aalborg v Manchester United Champions League Group match.]

'And in front of the United defence is the evergreen, or should that be ever-ginger, Paul Scholes...'

[Alan Green during Manchester United v Portsmouth.]

⚽ TANNOY TALES

While the supporters, if not the players, earn kudos for their catalogue of songs, the mystical folk on the loud-speaker systems have been known to indulge in football banter from time to time. While we shift from side to side in the freezing cold, waiting for the match to start, the comedians-in-waiting have graced stadia up and down the country... and indeed the world.

From as far as Australia, and a match between Wellington Phoenix and Perth Glory, the announcer warns:

'If you appear mashed, smashed or totally plastered

you will not be allowed into tonight's game.'

Chelsea announcer braces himself for a Champions League night at Stamford Bridge:

'And now the Olympiakos team sheet... wish me luck!'

[With the Greek giants including Zewlakow, Patsatzoglu and Djordjevic in the team, he needed all the luck he could get.]

Next a hilariously half-arsed request from the announcer at a Rochdale v Darlington game in 2009:

'Will Mr ******* please go to the club office immediately, your wife is in labour – you need to ring her, yeah?'

The Walsall announcer describes Cheltenham's decision to substitute Elvis Hammond:

'A substitution for Cheltenham means Elvis is leaving the building.'

More from the Walsall man, clearly loving the half-time limelight during a clash against Leyton Orient:

'I'm a big fan of the Orient, but to be honest I prefer

Pye Green Cantonese as they do a bostin' Singapore fried rice.'

Creepy crawlies at Eastbourne v Burton Albion:

'If anyone has a good knowledge of beetles – the insect, not the band – could they please make themselves known to us.'

Gillingham welcome Andy Barcham to the Priestfield Stadium, on loan from Tottenham:

'On loan from Tottenham so that he can feel what three points is like – Andy Barcham!'

[Spurs were bottom at the time.]

A short story from Wycombe v Brentford:

'Would the owner of the Vauxhall, registration number XXXXXX, please report to the nearest steward as you have left the handbrake off and it has rolled into the car behind you.'

Moments later...

'Would the owner of the Ford Fiesta, registration number XXXXXX, please also report to the nearest steward as yours is the one that has been hit.'

At least those unfortunate owners had a car...

'To the linesman in front of the stand, your car has been stolen. Does anyone know the number for a cab firm?'

[Announcement heard at non-league Ilford.]

As if Coventry defender Ben Turner's own-goal wasn't bad enough, the Preston public address system rubbed further salt into his wounds:

'Scoring his first goal for Preston North End, Number 20, Ben Turner!'

Doing his best to drum up some half-time excitement:

'Bolton nil, Blackburn nil – oh the joy. Anyone got a spare tin of paint so I can watch it dry?'

Followed by...

'Get ready to take a loan out for your pie and pint!'

[It didn't get much better. The game finished 0–0.]

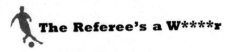

Horribly premature...

'This is a message for the Cardiff City fans; please can you leave your seats where they are, we may need them for the play-offs!'

[Announcer at Cardiff City's last home game of the season in 2009. The Blues fans should have taken a seat as a souvenir – Cardiff missed out on the play-offs by a single goal.]

You heard all about referee-baiting in the X-Rated section, but here's a slightly less offensive put-down to the error-prone official Stuart Atwell, heard at a match between Brentford and Notts County in 2009:

'And at half-time it's Brentford nil, Notts County one. Can any QUALIFIED refs please make themselves known to the nearest steward, thanks.'

Simple but effective:

'For those fans travelling on the away supporters' coach, please be advised that it has broken down.'

[Announcement at Aldershot v Dagenham and Redbridge, followed by loud cheers from the Shots fans.]

As a few men tried to break into the boardroom during Mansfield's home match against Rotherham: 'Can the people trying to break into the boardroom please be aware you are on CCTV.'

This announcer, speaking before Plymouth's clash with Burnley, raises a fair point:

'There's a mustard-coloured Peugeot in the car park, registration XXXXXX. You've left your windows open. Chances are if your car is a mustard colour you want it to be nicked, but just to let you know.'

A blindingly obvious reminder to Walsall fans:

'The next match here at the Banks' Stadium is on New Year's Day, which this year falls on 1 January.'

An ominous half-time warning at Colchester's match with Leicester:

'There is a no-smoking policy in all parts of the Layer Road ground. Anyone who is caught smoking will be taken away, strapped to an electric chair and electrocuted until they are dead. Thank you.'

Colchester announcer does his best to beat his previous warning, at half-time in their clash with Crystal Palace:

'There is a no-smoking policy at Layer Road. Anyone caught smoking will be taken to a darkened room, where they will be imprisoned for 27 hours and forced to listen to Will Young records for all of that time. Thank you.'

Oh dear...

'Please stand for the national anthem of the Republic of Northern Ireland.'

[Heard before England's Under-21 clash against the Republic of Ireland.]

⚽ BRILLIANT BANNERS

You may not know Manchester United fan Mick Groom – who's watched them in over 30 countries – but you will definitely know his banner:

UNITED, KIDS, WIFE – IN THAT ORDER.

Aston Villa fans rub it in as Newcastle are relegated, despite the efforts of Geordie 'Messiah' Alan Shearer:

WHO'S YOUR NEXT MESSIAH... ANT OR DEC?

Jubilant Everton fans unfurl tribute to Tim Cahill

following the Toffees' FA Cup semi-final win over Manchester United:

SUPERMAN WEARS TIM CAHILL PYJAMAS.

Football fans can be fickle. If you're winning, the manager is a God, lose and chants of 'OUT! OUT! OUT!' invariably spring up. But when Aston Villa were suffering under David O'Leary, the Villa Park faithful were eager to make it clear they were not blowing hot then cold:

WE'RE NOT FICKLE. WE JUST DON'T LIKE YOU.

Ouch!

Following the Heysel tragedy in 1980, it would be fair to say Juventus supporters hate Liverpool. The fiery Italians made their feelings clear during a Champions League match at the Stadio Delle Alpi in 2005:

YOU ARE MORE UGLY THAN CAMILLA.

Galatasaray's infamous:

WELCOME TO HELL.

[Hell? HELL?! They obviously haven't tried the Victoria line in rush-hour.]

The Referee's a W****r

Southampton slipped into League One following a dire Championship campaign in the 2008/09 season. Financial mismanagement meant they began the next season on minus ten points, hence this banner:

SHAME CARLSBERG DON'T DO BOARDS
OF DIRECTORS.

[If they did...]

Fans of LA Galaxy were not happy with a certain Mr Beckham upon his return to America following a loan spell at AC Milan. In his first game back, Becks was booed and almost had a fight with an irate Galaxy fan. Clearly furious with his lack of loyalty, the supporters spelled it out to the former England captain:

GO HOME, FRAUD
HERE BEFORE YOU. HERE DESPITE YOU. HERE AFTER YOU.

⚽ THE CHANT LAUREATE

In 2004, Jonny Hurst became the Premier League's chant laureate. He beat 1,500 rivals to the £10,000-a-year post with his song for Aston Villa striker Juan Pablo Angel. Hurst, a Birmingham fan, was responsible for coming up with new chants and

was paid double the salary poet laureate Andrew Motion received.

His winning song, which quite frankly had nothing on Manchester United's tribute to Park Ji-Sung or 'Two Andy Gorams', was sung to the tune of Barry Manilow's 'Copacabana':

His name is Angel
And he's a show boy
An Alice band keeps up his hair
Juan Pablo from Col-om-bi-air
He came to Villa
To be a winner
He succeeded overnight
Our very own Angel Delight
Just hear the Villa roar
With each Juan Pablo score
We've got him on a four-year deal
But we still want more
At the Villa, at Aston Villa
The greatest club west of Manila
At the Villa, at Aston Vi-lla
Football and passion
All ranges of fashion
At the Villa, we have it all
La-la, Aston Vil-la-la
Aston Vil-la-la-la
Vil-la-la-la

Self-employed solicitor Hurst did not get the adulation he wanted. Fans thought it was another attempt to cash in on the beautiful game and make the atmosphere more corporate-driven. Others thought he was a bit of a plank to be dreaming up songs for Aston Villa when he supported their arch-rivals Birmingham.

Football fans don't want a man telling them what to sing and how to sing it. We want freedom of expression, the chance to salute our heroes and slate our foes. Gherkins, porno flicks, advertising boards and unfit referees have all been the target of terrace appreciation and that is what makes the culture of the football song so wonderful.

We make our pilgrimages to Huish Park, London Road, Old Trafford and KitKat Crescent because we need some escapism in our lives.

For 90 minutes we can live for the moment, embrace every pass, howl at every foul and put our arms round a complete stranger while blasting the opposition fans through the medium of 'My Old Man's a Dustman'.

Yes, some of the chants are disgraceful, but amid a cacophony of noise and testosterone, we lose track of our emotions and of what can be considered acceptable.

So, the journey is over.

We can see you sneaking out!
We can see you sneaking out!
But before you do:
For £9.99 of your hard-earned cash you've
witnessed chip butties, tributes to Michael Jackson,
celery, lap dancers, a fat Paris Hilton, Woolworths,
queers, poached eggs, deep-fried pizzas, pineapples,
schizophrenia, tits, adultery, lasagne, dogs, prisons,
testicles, frogs, fake accents and more.

So I hope you'll agree that this book is:

Not a waste of money! Not a waste of money!